Marshal Arjan Singh, DFC
Life and Times

Marshal Arjan Singh, DFC

Life and Times

Group Captain Ranbir Singh (Retd)

Ocean Books Pvt. Ltd.

ISO 9001:2015 Publishers

Published by
Ocean Books (P) Ltd.
4/19 Asaf Ali Road,
New Delhi-110 002 (INDIA)

ISBN 978-81-8430-627-9
Marshal Arjan Singh, DFC
Life and Times

Edition
2019

Price
₹ 400.00 (Rs. Four Hundred only)

Printed at
Narula Printers, New Delhi

CONTENTS

PREFACE

Armed Forces are a pretty precedence based force. We do things the way they have been done, and that makes it rather difficult for us to change or accept a change. On the positive side, we are always propelled to emulate our legends and try to follow their footsteps. Superiority of IAF is largely due to quality of its manpower among the finest in the world, and we owe it to our legends who set exciting challenges for us to live up to.

You must have heard about the Keelor brothers—the Sabre Bashers of 1965 fame. Well, their story and behind it, there are thousands of stories and records that the public will never see or hear. The IAF is in action during peace and war, every day, every night, over the desert, plains, mountains and in all latitudes, with its vital genius for the rejection of formal speech. We take all our deeds and acts for granted. Results are meant to be achieved, we achieve them. Jobs are meant to be done; we just do them. The hazards, well, they are all in the day's work.

One simple result of this attitude of ours is that the achievements, even the landmarks in the history of IAF have got recorded in language crisp and business-like and perishable as a cardbox as far as future historians are concerned who may like to eulogize. Well, our records simply record a job that was to be done and we did it. Our deeds, exploits, feats of valour and so on lie hidden behind colourless communiques and factual broadcasts.

Of course, undoubtedly, the flatness and the lack of heroic touch in the recorded history of our achievements, is wholly attributable to the IAF. The men of the IAF are largely inarticulate. They rather prefer anonymity. We tend to speak of our most exceptional achievements in terms of understatement. To find a pilot who will tell you the story of a combat with simplicity, directness and lack of embarrassment is a rare thing.

What the IAF does and what the IAF says about what it does are different things. The fact that our achievements have not so far been recorded with outstanding objectivity, force and imagination is due to pilots, for the most part, cannot write, writers, for the most part, cannot fly. The day we get a fusion of these qualities in one person, we can get a real picture of IAF in action.

To the public, the most glamorous and the attractive is the fighter pilot. The reasons are again simple. His actions are seen as the triumph of individuality. He is engaged in a dangerous occupation.

A large part of our adventures cannot be called heroics. They are examples of fantastic fortunes and misfortunes which happen to any pilot, any day, anywhere. A fighter pilot's career is remarkable because it brings such a succession of events any one of which might have been his death. An indomitable stoicism, the spirit of apparently careless fatalism and a passion for flying are an important part of a fighter pilot's make-up.

This book is our humble tribute to one of our finest living legends, Marshal Arjan Singh.

D-72, Sector-21
Noida-201301
Tel: 91-4532809

Ranbir Singh

1

GREAT HONOUR TO THE IAF

Air Chief Marshal Arjan Singh, DFC, who retired 33 years ago as the Chief of the Air Staff of the Indian Air Force was made the first ever 'Marshal of the Air Force' in recognition of his extraordinary services on Friday January 25, 2002. With this new rank, equivalent to a Field Marshal in the Army, Arjan Singh joins Field Marshals Sam Manekshaw and KM Cariappa, in getting the highest rank in their service.

Marshal Arjan Singh, 82 years young, had said with his trade-mark smile which hasn't changed over the years, and has never failed to win you over instantaneously, "The Government has given a great honour to the IAF. I am very happy." He had gone on to add with all the humility and softness as has been his style, "This is a recognition of the standing of the Air Force, which is illustrated so dramatically by its role in the Gulf War and the Campaign in Afghanistan." In a lighter vein he had said, "I am looking forward to wearing uniform again after 32 years. I still fit into the uniform that I wore the day I retired, but I will have to get a new one since the attire has changed."

As Marshal of the IAF, he will now wear the uniform with five stars and four stripes and one band, that is one more than the Air Chief Marshal. The Marshal's rank has been bestowed on Air Chief Marshal Arjan Singh for leading the Air Force (IAF) in September War with Pakistan in 1965.

□

The Times of India had carried a one column news on the front page combined with the news of death of three security personnel on December 13, 2001. Perhaps, the Editorial Staff had missed out the significance of this event. Of course, they didn't have the space even to carry his photograph in the esteemed paper.

Hindustan Times had been a bit more liberal and found the space for a brief write-up on page 13, along with a small photograph of the former First Couple of the IAF. We appreciate that.

The IAF did a splendid job on the late afternoon of September 01, 1965, when the massive Pakistani armoured thrust was within the whispering distance from the Akhnur bridge and poised to cut off the Pathankot-Srinagar highway. Yes, it was one of the Finest Hours when we had gone and blunted the Pakistani Armoured thrust and stopped it in its tracks. We had just an hour in the late afternoon when the call came, and we didn't disappoint our Olive Green, Army friends. We will tell you more about this when we talk about the Operation Grand Slam. But for now the Government has after 37 years conferred this much awaited honour.

Tribune, Chandigarh, dated January 28, 2002 headlined the news item as, 'HONOUR DIMMED BY DELAY', and went on to say: "It is richly deserved but inexcusably delayed. This will be the rank of IAF Marshal on Arjan Singh." It further suggested: “It is time to see a pattern in honouring distinguished soldiers. IAF Marshal Arjan Singh should have been bestowed the highest honour a long while ago. He had earned it. And the country owed it to him. He was the first Air Chief Marshal, a rank equivalent to Army General and Navy Admiral. It was due to his work, planning and leadership. The Indian Air Force is very different today from what he came to lead and a big part of change is because of his character and also technological advancement. Why wake up so late in the day and award an honour in the evening of his life? The same thing happened to General Cariappa. He was elevated as Field Marshal years after General SHFJ Manekshaw was given the baton. A number of leading prominent men, political leaders, academicians and artists became Bharat Ratna either after their death or in old age. Why does the government need so much of time to assess their contribution to their respective field of activity? Take for instance, Kishore Amonkar. She has been around as an outstanding Hindustani classical singer for years; yet somebody woke up to her importance this year to list her name as a Padma Vibhushan awardee. A small mercy but a big mystery.”

☐

How Much We Care About Our Heroes?

Dan Quayle, an English poet had lamented:

“Our God and soldiers we like adore
Just at the brink of ruin not before
The danger past, both are alike requited
God is forgotten and soldier slighted.”

How True

I reproduce ‘An open letter to the Indian Air Force’,

written by Ajit Birdman (*Nom de plume* for an old Airman) which appeared at page 52 of Vayu 2000 Aerospace Review (1/97):

"Twenty-five years ago, December, 1971 was acclaimed as the finest hour (month) of the Indian Air Force: The Air Service had distinguished itself during the fortnight of 'All Out' Operations ranging from counter air attacks against enemy air bases and installations in the west and east, to the close air support to the Army in Kashmir, Punjab, Rajasthan, Gujarat and across the subcontinent in East Bengal, flying hundreds of Interception missions against enemy air intrusions, providing constant Combat Air Patrols (CAPs) over VAs/VPs, airlifting thousands of tons of vital stores, air dropping paratroopers in East Bengal, Heli-lifting troops across riverine obstacles even as the Army raced to enter Dacca.

So, twenty-five years later, at a hastily organized 'Vijay Diwas' on December 16, 1996, the nation marked the 25th anniversary of the triumph of India's All Arms with a near carnival atmosphere parade at National Stadium with motorcycle jinking, Para-jumping, limited air display by the Surya Kiran team and the purpose was served.

The media's criticism that the Leaders of the India's Military Triumph had been sidelined (at best) or forgotten (actually), the government's official spokesmen defended themselves stating that Field Marshal Manekshaw, Lieutenant General Jagjit Singh Arora and others had been invited but they chose to be away, the former (wrongly) rumoured as in Dacca, the latter at Fort William, Calcutta. In the event, Admiral S. Nanda (then Naval Chief) was seen amongst the last minute invitees at National Stadium, but with Air Chief

Marshal Pratap Chandra Lal, having passed away many years back, the next senior most Air Marshal Hari Dewan, AOC in C Eastern Air Command at Shillong, was relegated to the 'Back Benchers' and made to sit with relatively junior police and army officers. On being asked his views later, the Air Marshal simply said he wished he had never gone there. Shame (present) Government of India, Shame (present) Indian Air Force.

Various Commands, Corps, Divisions, Brigades and Units of the Indian Army reportedly celebrated their particular part in December, 1971 operations vigorously at their present locations. Eastern Command had their functions at Fort William Calcutta, the First Maratha LI at Saugar, and so many others.

How did Eastern Air Command mark the anniversary?

And No. 28 Squadron, whose MiGs fired those fateful rockets into the Governor's House in Dacca?

And No. 4 Squadron, whose MiGs 21s put the runways at Tezgaon and Kurmitola out of commission?

And No. 22 Squadron whose Gnats shot down three intruding Sabres over Boyra even before the war began?

And No. 10 Squadron whose Maruts interdicted enemy from LoC in the Sind desert?

And No. 20 Squadron whose Hunters shot down C 130 at Chaklala, Kohat and Mianwali?

And No. 26 Squadron whose SUs bore the brunt of OAS Missions?

And No. 35 Squadron whose Canberras set Karachi airport installations ablaze?

And No. 47 Squadron whose MiGs 21s shot down F-104s in the desert.

And No. 101 Squadron whose SU 7s turned the tide in Chhamb?

And Nos. 110/111 Helicopter units whose Mi 4s heli-lifted Gurkha riflemen across the Meghna in a daredevil effort?

And No. 222 Squadron whose SU 7s flew over 100 offensive missions in west.

And many others?

Well, we hope."

□

The Way to Do It

We have inherited all our customs and glorious traditions from the British with whom we had some close associations and there is no doubt that there is a lot we could have learnt from them, which unfortunately we did not. Let me share with you how the British treat their war heroes. This story had appeared in War News.

"Subedar Major (Honorary Captain) Umrao Singh, winner of a Victoria Cross, had gone to England in 1996 to attend biennial re-union of Victoria Cross holders. He was almost turned away from the entrance by the security guards as he had no ticket or invitation. A Brigadier passing-by had noticed that he was bearing a Victoria Cross Medal. He immediately took him to a place of honour.

Honorary Captain met the Queen Mother and other dignitaries while in England. He had an occasion to speak to Mr. John Major, the then Prime Minister of country, who spoke of his 'Privilege' by meeting Honorary Captain Umrao Singh. He had brought to his notice that the amount of annuity being paid to Victoria Cross awardees had remained stagnant for many years at a modest one hundred pounds sterling. The

Prime Minister announced the next day an enhancement to Pounds 1300 per annum."

My dear countrymen, this is the kind of faith the old timers have even today in the leadership of the old masters under whom they served during World War II or earlier.

□

A Year After the Fiasco

Let us see how we had fared a year after the latest Kargil Fiasco where the Media had a fairly close look at the life and the work style of our warriors. We had many *Netas* coming on record to say such nice and wise things about our fighters. What was the progress sheet after the Fiasco. I pen it for you from my notes taken during the period for you to judge how and how much we do care about our warriors?

More than a year after the Kargil War, little accountability has been fixed on how the Army ignored innumerable indicators about the imminence of the Pakistani intrusion across nearly 150 kms along the LoC. Senior officers had casually dismissed the invasion as a 'Localized Affair'.

The Chief of the Army Staff, General VP Malik, and the Northern Army Commander, Lieutenant General HM Khanna, were blissfully unaware of the extent of the infiltration.

At its peak, the infiltration had touched nearly two Brigades or 4000 to 5000 soldiers from Pakistan's Northern Light Infantry, and half that number at its lowest level towards the end of war in July, 1999. It was brought to a close by truly awesome bravery of Indian Officers and Jawans—and by Washington DC.

□

Earlier in the summer, General Malik had left on a 10

days trip to Eastern Europe, while Lt Gen Khanna had proceeded on vacation to Pune. All this while, in the meantime, General Pervez Musharraf, of course, was rather busy consolidating his position on the Himalayan Heights.

General VP Malik is reported to have told Journalist Gaurav Sawant as quoted in his book, 'DATELINE KARGIL':

"If the Chief of a million strong Army stops going out (abroad) when a patrol goes missing or a (ammunition) dump is targeted, then I will not be able to go to the toilet."

Says Sawant in the same book:

"The sham of army's tall claims of logistical war sickened me. The soldiers had no food to eat. For food they carried only *shakarparas*. For three days of fierce combat at heights above 16000 feet they carried only a litre of water, melting ice over the stove for the additional needs."

□

We made mistakes, plenty of them, right from the top to the bottom, the A to Z of military hierarchy. We failed to read the mind of the Pakistani Army Chief—General Pervez Musharraf, inspite of the fact that the General, at no stage, had concealed his contempt and the dislike for the country of his origin—India. It was a Diplomatic, Political and a Military Failure and we paid a heavy price for the complacency and misreading.

It was the initiations, innovations and the improvisations at the lower levels of the military leadership which, once again, as usual, rose to the occasion and provided the solutions where none existed. It was their daring and courage that had pulled the nation out of the mess created by the incompetent higher levels of command and control in all spheres.

We salute to them who fought and won at the

unbreathable heights under the most adverse circumstances, and despite all the neglect in all spheres of their activities—equipment, clothing, welfare and more—you name it and you will find that the Indian Jawan was grossly deficient on all fronts, and yet, they performed and put up a sterling performance—a performance to remember and be proud of.

BUT. The unanswered question is:

"Have we learnt our lessons?"

The answer, however much sadly is:

"NO." The general refrain is:

"The war is over, so is the sympathy and the concern."

It is about time that the nation, especially those who matter, realize that the Armed Forces are not looking for any sympathy or doles. They are too proud for that. Yes, they do feel happy and proud when the nation acknowledges their deeds of valour and sacrifices, and they do all that and more, out of a sense of duty. Similarly, they expect the nation to do its bit to ensure that their operational and welfare needs are met as a matter of national duty and not as a charity.

What irks them most is when the nation ignores them.

What hurts them is when the bureaucracy treats them shabbily in all walks of life.

What are the lessons from Kargil?

The Army Chief, General VP Malik had replied:

"There are many. But right now I would say that it is good that our country is giving so much respect to our martyrs. It helps in raising the morale while we are fighting. But I do wish that we respect the soldier and take care of both his operational as well as other needs during peacetime so that he doesn't have to become a martyr. If you start comparing a soldier to a policeman, paramilitary force or a good *chowkidar*, it hurts. It gives a feeling to the soldier that he is being neglected."

Well said.

Truly said.

Feelingly said.

It HURTS.

It hurts rather badly. But the harsh reality is that, as ever before, the disabled Jawans have been forgotten and left to fend for themselves, and more often than not, live in poverty and humiliation.

Nothing has changed.

A year after Kargil, the story is where we had left it in July 1999, with much hype and fanfare, not forgetting July 2000 when again the official hype was built up, money spent on non-essentials, and leaving the Jawans just as they were then.

The only silver lining I see, a year after Kargil is that, the nosey media which has had a fairly close encounter of a different kind in Kargil Front, happily, have not forgotten the humble, gritty Jawans with whom they had dared to spend time in their Bunkers, and had heard the real booms of guns and shells, and even shared the same emotions of fear and elation with them. They are the ones who have been quite willing to take up the just causes not only in the convenient urban areas, but have been quite willing to travel the distance to the remote rural areas for a just cause. Also noteworthy is the participation of the NGOs and private business houses in this worthy cause of doing their bit for the Jawans who need some help to live with their pride and honour intact. That is good news.

The Important Question

There is more to winning battles: the basic question that has not been debated, studied and analysed with a view to initiate the remedial measures in respect of all the wars we have fought since independence, and that includes the Kargil Fiasco also, is:

Why did it happen?

What lessons have we learnt?

Have we, indeed?

The candid answer is, 'NO'.

As soon as the Kargil Fiasco was over, as ever before, followed a much bigger Operation Cover-Up, in which the chairborne warriors have high stakes, and they make sure that the professionally competent are the ones who pay and account for the blunders, they are not responsible for.

We always forget the brave ones once the deed is done. The ministerial visits under the media glare elicit many grand promises which are never going to be honoured.

A year after the Fiasco it has been no different this time.

The fact is that the wise guys responsible for holding up the files which would have allowed atleast the basic equipment/ amenities to our soldiers, are back to their old games, and it is about time that they are exposed and punished and held accountable.

This is the tragedy of our system. No one seems to care for the brave Jawans who have to battle with the forces of nature, and the forces of the enemy, and have, yet, another bigger enemy within, the insensitive and uncaring bureaucracy in the Ministry of Defence. What we saw during the Kargil Fiasco was the most farcial and bizzare show of sympathy played day-after-day, till the show was 'On'.

A country which forgets and ignores its martyrs and gallant soldiers with such consummate ease, and yet slip into another slumber, war after war, is bound to come in the harm's way.

When the guns were booming in Kargil, the Indian Jawan was a part of the talk of the gilded cocktail circuits, because he was topical and fashionable to talk about. The real tormentors of our Jawans are the politicians and the bureaucrats who, in their desire to keep an upper hand, have always treated the defence callously.

Have we learnt our lesson this time?

Laments Mr Baljit Malik in *Hindustan Times* dated August 1, 2000:

"We are a year into Kargil. Kargil the Harakiri, the *Khudkushi* of two nations that have yet to grow up. War, in or out of uniform, is dirty three letter word. Yet, the irony is that, a war brings out the best in humans.

A year into Kargil, and it is still a riddle why Defence stalwarts are staggering in ceremonial farewells and remembrances only for a few well-deserved (?) war heroes. The *Raksha Mantri* and his minions have no time for the peasants, nomads, and the mules of Kargil without whom India would have become a sitting duck for the Islamic Hotheads across the border.

Despite inquiries, not even a single Court Martial for the dereliction of duty seems to have taken place. True (Brigadier) Surinder Singh, (Commander of Kargil Brigade) has been hounded from pillar to post. But then that is what happens when Generals are shaken on the saddle of their high rocking horse."

A year into Kargil, a year after a flurry of shopping jaunts to Europe by various Generals, the bureaucratic bottlenecks at Sena Bhavan and South Block have still not been able to bulldoze to facilitate even for woollen socks to reach the soldiers. Failure of Command, Control, Strategic Planning and Logistics have turned the peasant youth in the Army into cannon-fodder.

Apart from being a dirty three letter word, war is a very stupid method of providing employment and for ensuring a secure environment for socio-economic development. When there is no war, the Olive Green Army, the Air Force Blues, or the Fade Whites of Navy, amount to being a vast unaccounted waste of resources.

Patriotism

We are always told and reminded about patriotism and national spirit by our leaders out-of-uniform. One of the important aspects in the Defence Equation is to place the right man for the right job if you want to live up to the enviable slot of being second to none. Let me share with you a story narrated by a retired Air Marshal who does not wish to be quoted or identified.

"We were having a tea party in Zakir Hussain Mess with the Air Force Band regaling us with some evergreen tunes. Soon the band had struck the notes of Muhammad Iqbal's famous, *Sare Jahan Se Achchha*, which never fails to uplift the moods, and we were all merrily tapping our toes till suddenly we found that our honoured guest the *Rajya Raksha Mantri* was standing to attention with seriousness written all over him.

The Chief of the Air Staff (CAS) who was standing next to RRM, had no option but to stop tapping his toes and come to attention also, though he did not quite know 'WHY?' And once CAS comes to attention for whatever reason(s), everyone else does.

There was utter silence except for the band which itself was a bit confused for the sudden descent of silence and everyone in the gathering standing to attention. This had carried on for quite a few loaded moments till CAS had realized and correctly guessed the RRM's misconception, and discreetly whispered into his ears:

"Sir, this is not National Anthem."

HEROISM

Hero is endurance for one moment more.

WT Grenfell

Whosoever is heroic will always find a crisis to try his adage.

Emerson

No man is a hero to his valet. This is not because hero is not a hero, but because valet is a valet.

Epigram

2

PAST PERFECT: A BIOGRAPHICAL SKETCH

Marshal Arjan Singh was born at Lyallapur (now in Pakistan). He was educated at Montgomery and later at Government College, Lahore. Reminisces Marshal Arjan Singh:

"When I was selected for Air Force training in 1938, I had no idea whatsoever about the IAF except that I used to admire the aircraft flying over the area where I lived. In our batch three of us were selected, but one could not make the grade in flying and had, therefore, to be transferred to Indian Navy. Two of us passed out in December, 1939. Our training was cut short because of requirement of additional pilots for the war which had started three months earlier. It was only in January 1940, that I joined No. 1 Squadron, IAF, then based at Ambala."

Honours and accolades have come his way aplenty. Command of No. 1 Squadron at the height of Burma Campaign during the Second World War, a Distinguished Flying Cross (DFC) during the Burma Campaign, Chief of

Air Staff during 1965 War when the Indian Air Force provided the decisive edge that ensured eventual victory. Twenty years after he retired, he had the singular honour of being invited to take the parade at the Royal Air Force Academy at Cranwell, England, to commemorate the Fiftieth year of his commissioning. And now 33 years after his retirement he has been given the rank of Marshal.

Marshal Arjan Singh belongs to rare breed. Sprightly and always immaculately clad, he wears his age lightly. The manner in which he treats his dogs provides clue to his personality—kind, gentle, sympathetic and yet, ready to wield the stick if the occasion demands.

Generalship

Let us see what some of the ancient military thinkers had to say about good Generalship and the qualities of a good General.

- "It is the business of a good General to be serene and inscrutable, impartial and self-controlled.

  If he is serene, he is not vexed
  If he is inscrutable, he is unfathomable
  If he is upright, he is not improper
  If he is self-controlled, he is not confused."

Wang Hsi

- *"A General who regards his troops as infants, they will march with him into the deepest valleys. He treats them as his own beloved sons and they will die with him."*

Sun Tzu

- *"When Wu Ch'i was a General, he took the same food and wore the same clothes as the lowliest of his troops. On his bed there was no mat; on the march he did not mount his horse; he himself carried his reserve rations. He shared the exhaustion and the bitter toil with his troops."*

Tu Mu

- *"The General must be the first in the toils and the fatigues of the army. In the heat of the summer he does not spread his parasol nor in the cold of the winter don thick clothing. In dangerous places he must dismount and walk. He awaits until the army's wells have been dug and only then drinks; until the army's food is cooked before he eats; until the army's fortifications are completed, to shelter himself."*

Chang Yu

- *"If one uses kindness exclusively, the troops become like arrogant children and cannot be employed. Good Commanders are both loved and feared."*

Chang Yu

- *"Weapons are important but not decisive. It is the man's directing intelligence that counts most. In actual life we cannot ask for an invincible General. There have been few such Generals since ancient times. We ask for a General who is both brave and wise, who actually wins battles in the course of a war, a General who combines wisdom with courage."*

Mao Tse-Tung

□

No doubt that times have changed and the technology has brought about vast changes in the means and methods of modern warfare. But a close hard look at the qualities of a good General and Generalship as enunciated by the ancient military thinkers, hold good even today more so as we see the emerging Five Star life style of some Generals, which is bound to affect the important relationship between the officers and men.

What Others have to Say

Let us hear what others have to say about this old warrior for whom flying and the Indian Air Force has been his first love:

This is what *Statesman*, New Delhi, dated January 26, 2002, has to say about the grand old man:

"For both his professional and personal qualities he is held in the highest of esteem in international circles and is the only non-British personality to be twice invited to take the salute at the passing out parade at RAF Academy at Cranwell—from where he had himself graduated in the late 1930s."

□

Air Chief Marshal S Krishnaswamy, the present Chief of the Air Staff, says:

"He is the father-figure for the Indian Air Force, someone who not only contributed to the shaping up of the IAF but who could also be approached by successive Air Chiefs for advice on various matters. The honour would greatly boost the IAF's morale."

□

The Tribune, Chandigarh, dated January 28, 2002, writes: "It is richly deserved but inexcusably delayed, this will be the first thought of the Indians with a long memory on investiture of the rank of IAF Marshal on Arjan Singh. He led the Air Force in 1965 to a scintillating win over Pakistan. Even as Army columns got bogged down on this side of the Icchogil canal, Gnats and Sukhois dominated the sky and bottled up the Pakistani forces. Air Marshal Arjan Singh, that was his rank then and he became the first Air Chief Marshal the next year—led from the front. He was not holed up in a

moist air-conditioned room barking orders. He chose to fly his aircraft whenever he went inspecting bases, and airmen and officers admired him for his hands-on approach. He is a throwback to the pre-1947 days and rubbed proud shoulders with the Keelor brothers and several others from this part of the country."

□

"He came to airbase at Halwara to congratulate us on our performance," says former Air Chief Marshal NC Suri, who was then a young fighter pilot. "His leadership style was quite remarkable. He was one of the most benevolent Chiefs, yet very firm with orders. I congratulate the government on its recognizing the services rendered by a proud son of India. My only regret is that my efforts, while in office, to persuade the government to confer the rank of Marshal on Air Chief Marshal Arjan Singh, did not succeed. At that time government was not keen on having a Marshal. The rank seemed reserved for the Army."

□

Reminisces Group Captain BS Bakshi (Retd), a helicopter pilot:

I met Marshal Arjan Singh when he had taken over as AOC-in-C Operational Command, located in barracks at Palam Airport Area, and had come for a visit to Jorhat and Barrackpore. These airbases had become hub of supply dropping operations for posts in NEFA and later in support of the Army undertaking operations against Naga insurgents.

What I found remarkable about Marshal Arjan Singh was his dignified personality with a calm disposition which always inspired us all youngsters confidence and a desire to put in our best. He never missed an opportunity to mix with the younger lot as a human being.

In mid-fifties during a visit to Barrackpore he had walked into the Ladies Room of the Officer's Mess to wish a young lady who was waiting while her husband had gone to collect bread and eggs from the mess. He chatted with her and enquired about living conditions and shopping details in a manner as if he had come new and wanted to know about the place. Later her husband also joined the conversation. The young couple was totally ignorant about the tall, handsome officer till the husband saw him in uniform next morning.

During the same visit and night halt in Jorhat, he was totally at home in tented officer's mess and night shelter. He was not perturbed when he had found a cow sharing his tent during the cold night.

Another incident which indicates his practical and human approach was during 1963. A marriage party was arranged at Air House for the relative of Marshal Arjan Singh. Two days before the party, Air Vice Marshal Pinto was involved in a fatal helicopter accident near Poonch. The function was held to meet the family's obligation but without any lightings or music normally an integral part of Indian weddings.

In mid-sixties I had taken over the command of a Mi-4 Helicopter Unit. We were detailed to undertake Prime Minister Indira Gandhi's tours in UP hills and Orissa to visit the drought hit areas. In Mi-4 helicopter the cockpit is about 2 metres higher than the passenger cabin. I therefore used to send information about our position, important landmarks and latest news monitored on radio compass frequency on small slips of paper to the Prime Minister.

On April 1, 1967, I was one of the recipients for investiture parade for Vayu Sena Medal awardee for 1965

operations. After the parade Marshal met my father who was sporting NWFP headgear of *Kulla* and *Lungi* which attracted Marshal's attention. When he learnt that Pathan attired man was my father, he mentioned to him about the compliments paid by Prime Minister regarding the courtesy to keep her informed about the progress of flights in the noisy chopper.

During the high tea after the same Air Force Day cum Investiture Parade, my niece who was about three years of age, happened to be near the Marshal who bent down to have a little chat with her. She wanted to touch the medals on the Marshal's uniform, but couldn't reach them due to the height difference. Marshal Arjan Singh had correctly guessed her curiosity and desire, and picked her up and held her in his arms till she had inspected all his medals and touched them to her heart's content and given a broad smile of sheer delight.

In December 1997, I attended release of a book *Pakistan's Criminal Folly in Kashmir*, authored by my brother Chibber, in India International Centre. Marshal Arjan Singh had been invited for the function. In a polite conversation he had mentioned that he did not know the author personally, but an ex-serviceman undertaking a venture of this nature must get support from all of us. The sentiments at that age and stage speak volumes about what he has inside his visible personality—a true love and genuine feelings for the men-in-uniform.

□

Wing Commander SP (TAK) Khanna (Retd), had this brief encounter with Marshal Arjan Singh, which is etched in his memory:

"In 1959, I had gone up for a training sortie with Flying Officer Rana Gautam in Vampire Trainer Aircraft. We had taken off from Halwara Airbase, and had carried out some aerobatics and towards the fag end of the sortie during a low speed roll-of-the-top, our aircraft had juddered and got into incipient spin. It took us a while to realize that we were in an incipient spin. Inspite of the recovery action taken, the aircraft had continued to spin and also lost height continuously.

Rana had asked me to bail out. In the process of leaving the aircraft, my parachute strap had got stuck with a broken hook to the canopy. I was going around in the direction of the spin, half hanging inside and half outside with the parachute strap stuck with the broken hook. This none too-pleasant and unforgettable nightmare had carried on from about 14000 feet till 3000.

Mercifully, at about 3000 feet the aircraft had spun in the opposite direction and Rana had managed to push the aircraft in a dive, and she came out of the spin. I sat back in the cockpit holding the cockpit railing, and we made a safe landing. Air Marshal Arjan Singh who was then the AOC-in-C of Special Operational Command was immediately informed about the incident. He flew down to Halwara and gave me a hug and a pat on the back, and listened to my whole story over a cup of tea. He was very pleased by the recovery action taken and told the Squadron Commander to give me more spinning sorties to build up my confidence.

I can now say, how great a human being he is who had total faith in his aircrews and concern about their welfare and operational preparedness."

□

The Indian Air Force in its official handout on the occasion says: "Many officers and men who served with him still fondly remember the Marshal as a hands on, non-formal,

incisive and humane person, who flew himself to visit stations and units in his Canberra. He belongs to the breed of rare few individuals who had the difficult task of shaping the IAF not only in its nascent years, but also in several difficult periods. He saw the IAF carrying out its assigned operations in 1962 Sino-Indian War. He steered the 1AF through the 1965 War that was forced upon us. His stewardship ensured defeat of the adversary and his plans. He also guided the Air Force through the post 1965 embargoes and sanctions."

□

Life and Time

In recognition of the most valuable services to the Air Force and the Nation, the rank of Marshal of the Indian Air Force for life has been conferred on Air Chief Marshal Arjan Singh, DFC (Retd) with effect from January 26, 2002.

Air Chief Marshal Arjan Singh, DFC (Retd) was born on May 15, 1919 at Lyallapur. He was educated at Montgomery and later at Government College in Lahore. A tall well-built Sikh, he came from a distinguished family of Punjab. He was selected for flying training course at Cranwell in 1939 and was last of the Indian Air Force officers trained at this institution. In 1938, he was selected for pilot's training at Cranwell, UK and was commissioned as a pilot in Royal Indian Air Force in December, 1939. The first batch of Indian pilots was granted king's commission on October 8, 1932. In the later years nine more Indians were selected for flying training at Cranwell. They were Majumdar, Ranganathan, Prithipal Singh, Narendra, Habibullah Khan, Mehar Singh, RHD Singh, Surendra Nath Goyal and Arjan Singh. This comprised the total strength of officers in the Indian Air Force till 1939 when World War II began. He joined No.1 Squadron at Ambala, first on Wapiti aircraft and later converted to Hurricane aircraft. He took over as Commanding Officer of No. 1 Squadron in September, 1943. He was awarded the Distinguished Flying Cross in 1944, for his outstanding leadership in Burma Campaign during the World War II. At that point of time, the country was still under the British rule and for an Indian to be awarded such a high honour was indeed a matter of immense pride for the nation.

He was promoted to the rank of Wg Cdr in 1945 and attended the first course at Royal Staff College, Bracknell. After partition, as Gp Capt he commanded Air Force Station Ambala. In 1949, as Air Commodore, he was appointed Air Officer Commanding Operational Command and in 1952, he was appointed the Air Officer Commanding-in-Chief Operational Command. Subse-quently, he held key appointment of AOA, DCAS and VCAS from 1958 to 1964. In 1960, he was specially selected for the Imperial Defence College, UK (later named as the Royal College of Defence Studies).

He was appointed the Chief of the Air Staff in July, 1964 at the age of 44. He was the first Chief to be promoted to the rank of Air Chief Marshal in December, 1965. In recognition of his services of an extremely high order, and for his leadership during the 1965 War against Pakistan, Air Chief Marshal Arjan Singh was awarded the *Padma Vibhushan*, the second highest national award. He retired from the Air Force in July, 1969 at the age of 50. During his tenure as the Chief of the Air Staff, he brought about significant changes in the structure and functioning of the Air Force, to charter it towards a path of strong professional growth. His outstanding leadership groomed the Indian Air Force into one of the best

Air Forces in the world.

Even after retirement, Air Chief Marshal Arjan Singh has rendered distinguished service of an exceptional order to the nation for nearly two decades. During this period he held various important assignments, in each of which he served with exceptional success.

- Indian Ambassador in Switzerland 1971–74
- High Commissioner in Kenya 1974–77
- Member, Minorities Commission 1978–81
- Chairman, Indian Institute of Technology New Delhi 1980–83
- Director, Grindlays Bank 1981–88
- Lt Governor of Delhi State 1989–90

His inspiring career and high reputation have endowed him with a unique stature in society and has earned him the respect of the nation. Even till date, he associates himself with various welfare activities of the Air Force as a father figure of the service, which he nurtured from a fledgling status.

They say old Generals fade away. The nation has done itself proud by recognizing the meritorious services of one of its pioneering and intrepid military aviators—a true son of the soil during his life time. A befitting recognition of air power in these troubled time.

LIFE

Life is not dated merely by years; events sometimes are the best calenders.

Benjamin Franklin

Chief of Staff Committee Farewell to CAS (10.7.1969)

3

THE AIRBORNE CHIEFS

We had two Air Chiefs who could be truly called the Airborne Chiefs. The First was Air Marshal Sir Ronald Ivelaw Chapman (February 22, 1950 to December 9, 1951). The Air Marshal in his own unique way had rekindled the joys and thrills of flying amongst many of his Chairborne Commanders, who had found the Ten-to-Five routine an entirely satisfactory way of carrying on with their administrative duties based on the past experiences and laurels.

Air Marshal Chapman had different ideas. He was convinced that the only way to effectively administer an Air Force was if you kept in touch with flying because that is what an Air Force is meant to do. Besides, he also showed that the only way to enthuse others is through personal example. Rightly so. He has left this important lesson for the future generations to follow.

Air Marshal Chapman records in his Service Memories:

"Another important conclusion I came to soon after taking over was that, too many of IAF senior officers were quite content to become chairborne and float along on their reputation that they had once qualified for their wings. Instead of gathering them all at a conference and ranting at them on the subject, I resorted to a subtler-and for me a much pleasanter form of attack.

I discovered that in their photographic Reconnaissance Unit they had a number of Spitfires with the Griffon Engine (Spitfire PR MK XIs of No. 101PR Squadron). Although I had not flown that mark of Spitfire before, I mugged up the pilot's handling notes, and within a few weeks of my taking over, I used to sneak off to Palam airfield before breakfast and have half an hour or so of pleasure in one of these Spits.

The effect was ELECTRIC. This is precisely what I had intended. I had noticed that some of the more elderly officers were clocking up flying hours in one or another aircraft of their choice. Next I took to arriving by Spit whenever I felt it was within my capacity, to take a Passing Out Parade, or an AOC-in-C inspection. My ADC flew information with me in another Spit, and I had to undergo the ordeal of landing in front of a vast parade drawn up on the tarmac, and usually a host of parents and official visitors as well, I managed to get away with it, and just before the end of my tenure I flew one of their Jets–Vampire, with which they had just been equipped. This pleased them enormously, and on the eve of my final departure for England, at a rather formal ceremony at Delhi, I was duly presented by the Minister of Defence with the Indian Air Force pattern of wings, thus bringing my total with RFC, RAF, up to three. Even today, 25 years later when I met some senior officers of the present IAF, I was assured that I am still remembered as the C-in-C who kept the IAF in the Air."

Air Marshal Chapman concludes his memories with: "When I heard from the Air Ministry in London that I was to return to UK in December, 1951, to take up the post of Deputy Chief of Air Staff, I sat down and spread myself over three pages of full scape, pleading that I should be allowed to stay in India for another year to finish the job I had begun, as I think I put it."

To this he got a short shrift from CAS (Chief of Air Staff), Jack Slessor, who was the DCAS. It was to the effect that:

"You can tell Chaps that it's quite time that he finished gallivanting around India in his Spitfire and come back here to White Hall and get down to some real work."

□

An avid aviator all his serving years, Arjan Singh flew all types of aircraft in the IAF during his time, from its inception till the induction of Jets and Supersonics. Many officers and airmen who served during his tenure, still fondly remember him as a hands on, non-formal, incisive and a humane person, who flew himself to visit stations and units in his Canderra aircraft whenever the runway was available. Reminisces Marshal Arjan Singh:

"On the day I retired I had jumped into the cockpit of the MiG 21 to fly a fighter one last time. I knew that the Indian Air Force won't let me fly again." Such was his love for flying.

From the time he was commissioned in the Royal Indian Air Force in December 1939, he has flown 60 different types of aircraft. He flew the Westland Wapitis in North West Frontier Province chasing the Pathans and Hurricanes in Burma during World War II. His favourite aircraft has been the Canberra.

When Arjan Singh took over as the Chief of Air Staff he was categorized as operationally fit to fly all types of aircraft that were in service at the time including fast jet fighters. He had kept himself in flying trim by often going to the Flying Squadrons and flying with them doing the normal armament training. In fact, he was the first Air Chief of the Air Force fully operationally fit and capable of guiding and directing the services in any operations that were undertaken. He had grown up with the Air Force and had all the experience of his predecessors. He was a born leader to whom all ranks looked for guidance and direction. Such combination of qualities is rarely witnessed in any one person.

EXAMPLE

We do more good by being good than in any other way. ***Proverb***

Rules make a learner's path long, Examples make it short and successful. ***Epigram***

EXCELLENCE

Demand excellence and be willing to pay for it.

Graffiti

MARSHAL'S REMINISCENCES

4. The Number One—As I Knew It
5. Leadership In The Air Force
6. When On The Wings: From Marshal's Album Of Evergreen Memories
7. His Candid Views
8. Would You Do It Again?

A PRIDE OF TIGERS
'A' Flight No. 1 Sqn
Front row (standing) L to R: F/O Hafiz, F/L Gnaniovulu, F/O Talwar
Centre row (seated) L to R: F/O Prabhakar, F/O Rishi, P/O Sarkar, Capt Williams, S/L Arjan Singh DFC, F/O Dwarpalak, F/O Amber, F/L Rajaram DFC, F/O Rao DFC, F/O Gupta DFC
Standing (rear): F/O Kak DFC, F/O Pandit DFC

4

THE NUMBER ONE—AS I KNEW IT

I am writing this from memory about the one and the only Squadron I ever belonged to; I have never served in any other.

It was during the first week of January, 1940 that two Pilot Officers—Prithipal Singh and I—on finishing our flying training at the RAF College, Cranwell, joined No. 1 Squadron at Ambala, then commanded by Sqn Ldr (later 1st CAS as Air Marshal) S Mukerjee and equipped with Wapiti, Hart and Audax aircraft, thus completing its full establishment of pilots. The other senior pilots were Flt Lt AM Engineer (Aspy) (later CAS as Air Marshal) and Flt Lt Majumdar (Jumbo), a Flight Commander. A flight at Karachi for sea reconnaissance and air support called 'Q' Flt (for unknown reasons) under Flt Lt AB Awan and a flight at Fort Sandeman under Flt Lt Narendra for army support of Tochi Scouts had Westland Wapiti aircraft.

At the Royal Air Force Station, Ambala, the Tigers (No. 1 Squadron, IAF) were always competing, in a friendly way, with the RAF Squadron (No. 28) in every activity, both at work and play. We watched with a critical eye each others takeoffs and landings, bombing on the grass airfield (Ambala had no hard runway at that time) with practice bombs weighing 8 or 11 pounds. Sometimes, that event was also watched by the ladies of the Air Force. In bombing our accuracy was invariably a little better than that of the RAF Squadron.

In other aspects also the IAF was always trying hard to compete and prove itself; this attitude continued throughout the 1939-45 war and gave our officers and airmen much confidence and determination. In the Officers' Mess, someone had introduced a beer drinking competition. The Squadron officers lined up facing each other on a long table with a pewter beer mug full to the brim in front. The mugs, after drinking, had to be turned upside down on the table in a relay race; speed and cleanliness of the table decided the winner after two or three rounds.

The systematic training in flying, strict discipline on the ground and in the air and participation in team sports in the Squadron served me well throughout my time in the IAF and, in fact, thereafter. I had to wait my first solo in the Squadron till I had learnt to clean the aircraft properly and till I was tested and cleared for solo flying by the Flight Commander, the Adjutant and ultimately the Squadron Commander; this was, by the way, on the type I was trained on. The discipline and hierarchy were well maintained. Once in a standing interview with the Adjutant I put my hand on his table inviting a severe shout to remove it. Even in the mess seniority was the form but in the houses of our married officers I was generously and informally entertained. The participation of all officers, high or low—was compulsory in team sports. In my opinion, that is where one gets tough in mind and body, learns team spirit and gets to know one's colleagues in formations like a Squadron.

No. 1 Squadron had gained vast experience and credit (AM Engineer got DFC and many others Commendations) in operations on the North-West Frontier before the real war in the East started. The Japanese military build-up, threat and attack on the countries of South East Asia gave the Indian Air Force a tremendous opportunity to expand fast and thereafter gain operational experience in modern warfare and against a formidable enemy. No. 1 Squadron went to Burma under the command of 'Jumbo' Majumdar with Lysander aircraft in 1942 and undertook some daring operations against heavy odds earning a good name for the Squadron and a DFC for its CO. The Squadron retreated to India along with the ground forces under pressure of the Japanese advance.

On returning to India with a soaring reputation, it was equipped with Hawker Hurricane aircraft in 1942 at Tiruchirapally under the command of Subroto Mukerjee; I was the Squadron Adjutant. The Squadron moved to Kohat under a different CO. It soon suffered some loss of reputation and, in a sudden move, the CO was removed about the middle of 1943 and I, then a Flt Cdr, was asked to take over. After some time, the Squadron boys—pilots, technicians and others—were keen and confident to get back into operations against the Japanese. In early December 1943, Field Marshal Sir Claude Auchinleck (then C-in-C of all Defence Forces in India) paid a visit to the RAF Station, Kohat. On request, I was given an interview where I advocated the intense desire and claim of No. 1 to go into operations. The Station Commander (an RAF Wg Cdr) supported my request. To the immense joy of the Squadron chaps we received orders, within a week of the FM's visit, to proceed to Imphal without delay.

The danger to India was apparent; the Japanese forces were pressing hard on the Akyab and Imphal Fronts, the two routes they had planned for a grand entry into India. They had a vain hope that Indian Defence Forces would cooperate. The Japanese plan was frustrated and the Tigers of No. 1 had a significant role to play in that task. The Squadron arrived, on the New Year day of 1944, at the Imphal airfield, the only one with a *pucca* runway and stayed there for over a year. Its task was to protect and support our Army, including the British and African troops. To achieve that, offence being the best defence in most situations, it flew offensive sorties every day (except on really bad weather days) of the year attacking with bombs, guns and rockets Japanese camps, transport, tanks, guns and generally everything seen moving on their lines of communication. We met with a certain amount of success as later discovered from photographs taken by us and the wrecked weapons of war left behind by the Japanese on retreat. We, at rare times, encountered the Japanese Zero fighter, a good air combat aircraft but the Hurricane was ideal for ground attack.

No. 1 Squadron went to Imphal with about 20 pilots but only 4 of the original lot returned after a year's operations without a break; that was sad and heart-rending. The Squadron, in these operations, earned nine DFCs and one MBE. Such a long period on operations was not equalled by any other Squadron—IAF or RAF—during World War II in South Asia. The Japanese were, however, successful in laying siege of the Imphal Valley. All the Air Force units except 2 Squadrons—one RAF and the other, No. 1—were evacuated as enough fuel and other logistics required for air operations could not be flown into the Valley.

The intensive air operations were supported by a very high serviceability, often 100%. The rule then was that if an aircraft could be made serviceable for flying by the morning it was reported as serviceable to the RAF Group. This was achieved by the Squadron personnel under Sqn Eng Officer Flt Lt Ram Singh (who earned MBE) by carrying out repairs and engine changes at night unlike the RAF Squadrons in the Valley. However, many doubted its veracity till it was tested by a sudden operation. One day, at half an hour's notice, we were asked to attack a Japanese column entering the Valley from the hills. All sixteen aircraft of No. 1, fully loaded with appropriate armaments, got airborne and attacked the Japanese troops with such success that they started retreating. Many written accounts (both by IAF and RAF) have given credit to No. 1 for foiling that serious attempt by the Japanese Army to capture the Valley.

It is not possible to give a detailed account here of the air operations carried out by No. 1 Squadron on the Burma Front during 1944. But I do remember with gratitude that each pilot flew about 2 sorties a day except one day of every week; that imposed much physical and mental fatigue on all members and, particularly, the pilots. Flying over the dense forests of Burma was psychologically strenuous, navigation (map reading) was difficult and successful forced landing, almost impossible. Landing by parachute meant no escape from the thick jungle or the snakes, leeches and animals inside. A few pilots could not bear the accumulated strain and had to be withdrawn from flying and sent back. Appreciating the difficult operational and living conditions I did not take notice of any minor beat-up or indiscipline and had no occasion to reprimand anyone.

The inevitable order came after my full year at Imphal and I handed over the Squadron to the Senior Flt Cdr Flt Lt R Rajaram, DFC (later Vice Chief as Air Marshal) on 1st January 1945 and reported to Air HQ.

Looking back, I have no hesitation in saying that was my best time in the IAF except for the big loss of my flying colleagues who sadly never returned home. They gave their best to firmly establish the IAF in its present glory and I pay my homage to them. Whilst greeting the Tigers' in their Diamond Jubilee Year I have no doubt that they will, in future, continue and further enhance the great traditions and achievements of the 'Number One'.

NOSTALGIA

Nostalgia is recalling the fun without re-living the pain.

Graffiti

Nostalgia is halfway house by which you love the past and the sweet things in it without actually committing yourself to the nonsense that life was better then.

Henry Mitchell

5

LEADERSHIP IN THE AIR FORCE

(The story of IAF has been a glorious saga built over a period of time by many magnificent men in their not-so-magnificent flying machines. They struggled against odds, risked their lives at times and set personal examples that inspired others to follow them in their footsteps. In the process, many came to be viewed as true leaders; some of them even became legends. In this interesting article, ACM Arjan Singh sums up the qualities of a leader, with particular reference to Air Force. Needless to mention that his own sterling qualities of leadership have become a byword in Air Force.)

No one has really defined leadership to the satisfaction of all. It is not a scientific or a mathematical problem that can be quantified; it is a human problem. It would, therefore, have different yardstick and requirement at various levels and under different situations. In dealing with the subject I may give some personal examples with the hope that it would not be considered as my ego problem.

The first problem of leadership in the Air Force I faced

was at a fairly young age, about 22, when I became a Flight Commander in the rank of Flt Lt. The Flight had about 8 or 9 pilots, all in the rank of Flying Officer or Pilot Officer except the Flight Commander. As one of the officers in the Flight in the rank of Flying Officer, I was very close to all the pilots. We consumed much tea in the crew-room and took part in all sports together. When I became the Flight Commander, I discovered that the bonhomie could not last long. I had to give many orders, arrange flying programmes, etc., and enforce discipline both on the ground and in the air. On what I thought were minor matters, my old 'pals' used to show resentment. I soon discovered that I had few friends left in my Flight. That was an eye-opener and quite a shock. I then began to realize that it is very lonely and cold at the top—at any top—and this kind of isolation increases as we go up the ladder in command appointments. What I experienced as Flt Cdr was a lesson for me and it served me well in later command appointments.

In this respect, there is just another point I want to make and that is, a Commander being too social and friendly with some and not so with others. In that situation, the Commander is likely to be accused, perhaps in a whisper, of having favourites. That can do much harm to cohesion in the unit. That was always one of the delicate problems I had to face in various appointments. The fact of life is that meek and mild officers with a gift of the gab are pleasant company; they try to overcome their professional weaknesses through social contact. On the other hand, the efficient officers are strong willed and can hold their own in discussions even expressing views contrary to those of the boss. Even though they may temporarily hurt the Commander's ego, they are more useful to the service and, in fact, to him also in making a success of his command. The Commander has to face this aspect while submitting reports on his officers. It is always difficult to give an adverse report to 'good' chaps. My experience is that professional ability with integrity is not always compatible with what may be termed as goodness in a 'nice' man. I had to retire some very 'nice' officers after the 1965 war. A commander must be honest to himself and recognize professional merit whatever the other considerations may be.

Air Force Leadership

I would define an Air Force leader as a man whom his subordinates would follow with confidence and are prepared to undertake the most hazardous operations and other tasks even at the risk of supreme sacrifice. What are the various qualities that a leader should possess? An ignorant man about his profession can not be a good leader. Whatsoever smartness with elegant manners he may possess, he would not be able to fool his subordinates; they would, sooner than later, know his bluff and worth. It is therefore essential to acquire, through study and hard work, knowledge to perform various tasks. And what is more important, the service officers and Commanders must keep themselves up-to-date in every aspect of the Service; otherwise, they will not command respect, nor would they understand the intricate problems and technology of today and carry out their duties properly.

In the Air Force, the actual fighting is done by a small number of flyers. One must be able to understand their problems, difficulties and gauge their capabilities. That is possible only if the Commander has knowledge of the tools with which those flyers are required to do the job. I have always strongly felt that all Commanders should keep themselves fully up-to-date and fly the aircraft which they are going to deploy during a war. The young officers do not expect the very senior Commanders to fly as well as they do and use the weapons like them who are in almost daily practice to do so. They also know that during a war very senior Commanders may not be allowed to operate over the enemy territory. If a senior Commander flies and is seen to be taking more or less, similar risks it is a great morale booster throughout the service. Moreover, his decisions would closely relate to the capabilities of the flyers and the aircraft. That would produce better results with minimum cost to the Air Force and the country.

Character

This is another quality which is difficult to define precisely. It should, in my opinion, consist of integrity, moral strength and willpower to stick to the principles of justice and fair play. A man of character will avoid favouritism and discourage sycophancy. A good leader is able to stick to decent values and his principles even at the cost of discomfort to him at times. The strength of character is important in the Air Force as otherwise it may unnecessarily risk and endanger a number of highly valued lives. Air Chief Marshal Sir Hugh Dowding of the RAF, as AOC-in-C Fighter Command, refused to send more fighter Squadrons to France during World War II to resist the German advance, a hopeless task in that phase of the war, even though Prime Minister Winston Churchill was quite adamant. Churchill, being all powerful, could have removed him from the Command. However, Dowding was not prepared to give-in against his considered judgment and stuck to his point. It is now recognized that, that action ensured the success of the RAF in the Battle of

Britain which was, at one time, a touch and go affair. Dowding showed strength of character for the sake of Britain and the RAF.

Personal Leadership

At some levels of Command in the Air Force it is of utmost importance to display personal leadership by exposing oneself to danger first of all. The old examples which come to my mind are those of Wg Cdr 'Jumbo' Majumdar and Air Cmde Mehar Singh. Majumdar, as CO of 1 Sqn, led many attacks on vital Japanese targets in 1942 in Burma against known Japanese superiority in fighter aircraft at that time. Mehar Singh himself landed at Poonch under enemy fire and Leh on the quite unprepared landing ground before asking other pilots to do so. In life itself and particularly that in the Air Force, one has to face many adverse situations. It is a desirable trait of character to absorb such adverses. I had many such occasions even as a junior officer. I learnt to live with them. I admitted my faults like unauthorised low flying and did not give excuses to justify my action. One should always try to do one's best, work hard, be honest to oneself and be firm, fair and impartial. That, in my opinion, is the way to do well and enjoy life in our Air Force.

LEADERSHIP

No one leads the orchestra without turning his back to the crowd.

Graffito

Precepts lead but examples draw.

Proverb

Old friend and Squadron Mate, Air Marshal Ashgar Khan, Pakistan Air Force Chief, during his visit to India on November 07, 1964, little knowing that in less than a year they will be fighting each other during the September War in 1965.

6

WHILE ON THE WINGS: FROM MARSHAL'S ALBUM OF EVERGREEN MEMORIES

The first flypast in independent India was carried out without any rehearsal on 15 August, 1947 when the Prime Minister Pandit Jawaharlal Nehru unfurled the new national flag on the western ramparts of the Red Fort. The flypast consisted of 12 Tempest aircraft. It was led in three sections of four aircraft each. The aircraft flew through many flocks of birds and it was sheer chance that none was hit. Over that densely populated area any accident could have had quite disastrous results. Due to these dangers, no flypast has been carried out over the Red Fort thereafter.

During World War II, the Air Force was having trouble in getting recruits in adequate numbers for pilot and other training. To make people air-minded 'a display flight' was started with a distinguished pilot, the late Wg Cdr Majumdar as its Commanding Officer. He was killed doing aerobatics in a display over Lahore. On his death, I took over and gave acrobatic displays with a single Harvard aircraft. How times have changed and skills improved over these years! The Thunderbolts led by Wg Cdr Brar and equipped with 8 Hunter jets put up an acrobatic display which could be the envy of any air force.

What a change from the days when I went to the Royal Air Force College, Cranwell, England in 1938! Before I left for my flying training I was given advice by relatives and friends to 'fly low and fly slow'. During training we had more accidents due to these two causes, that is flying slow and stalling and flying low and hitting trees and electric cables even with those World War I vintage airplanes.

The World War II started on September 3, 1939, when I was still under training at Cranwell. The same night there was an air raid alert and we spent most of the night sitting in an open trench. Later it was discovered that it was an English aircraft returning from France but declared hostile by the control set-up in panic.

After commissioning, I stayed on in England for further training during the so-called 'twilight' period of the war. However, early in 1940 I joined No. 1 Squadron, the only Squadron the Indian Air Force had. The build-up of this Squadron had been really slow, adding two or three pilots each year. It was commanded by Sqn Ldr Mukerjee, the first Indian to command this unit. The Squadron was in a delicate position as there was always an attempt to compare it, at times with some built-in prejudices, with British Air Force units based at the station. I remember that for the first fortnight with the Squadron, I was not allowed to fly an aircraft but only clean it. Within a few days it was sparkling in the sun. When a decision was taken presumably by the Squadron Commander that I might fly the aircraft I had flown during my training days, I was tested by three Squadron pilots including himself before giving me the green light to go solo. Such care and thoroughness was responsible for maintaining high standards in the Squadron.

With the war on in Europe, there were signs of the dark clouds of war building up in the East. The build-up of the defence forces in India had started to meet the challenge in the East and thereby help the war effort in Europe and the Middle East. Additional facilities for training pilots were built up and the Indian Air Force had to be given some operational training. For that purpose, the North West Frontier was an ideal place where the Pathans had continued their valiant fight against the British and Indian troops for many decades. One also got the feeling that the British were not keen to stop fighting as it gave them a place for battle experience. It was with this aim in view that No. 1 Squadron, of which I was a member, moved to the North West Frontier. We all had high regard for the Pathan. We considered them very honourable men and courageous fighters. The Air Force went into action only when movement of our troops supporting our forward posts was interfered with. At times Pathans were using modern arms captured from our troops and they used them with great effect. I had personal experience of this when I was flying in support of our troops guarding a road to a military camp. When I was diving and firing my machine-guns, the engine fluttered and then stopped. I had some extra speed, so I climbed up and looked around for a place where I could put down the aircraft with the dead engine. I ultimately landed in a dry river bed. When our troops arrived, they counted 16 bullet marks in and around the engine. The Pathans, firing from captured machine-guns, had scored handsomely and downed an aircraft. Such cases were not common but we had many aircraft returning with a couple of bullets. While we were getting some operational training on the Western frontier, the war in the East was approaching our borders. The Japanese were advancing fast and there was much panic in India. The defence forces in India were hardly prepared to face a well-equipped enemy. However, frantic efforts were in hand in India and the Indian Air Force was equipping, training and expanding to meet that threat. No. 1 Squadron, under the command of that daring officer Sqn Ldr Majumdar, was despatched to Burma to help our retreating army to delay the Japanese advance. From then onwards the Indian Air Force was fully engaged on the eastern front, the climax being reached during 1944. Though I was flying to Burma mostly for communication work during 1942, it was not till 1944 that I got fully involved in the war on the eastern border.

I was commanding No. 1 Squadron at Kohat when towards the end of 1943 we got orders to move to Imphal in the first week of January 1944. Though based in India, most of our flying was over Burma. Flying over thick tropical jungle is quite unnerving. The pilots knew that in case of engine trouble, the chances of survival were rather remote. I remember that we were given a number of lectures on how to survive in the jungle. Getting out of a thick jungle is quite a problem as one loses orientation. Another problem is food. Though we carried some rations, these could be lost during a crash or parachuting. So we also learnt how to kill and live on snakes. And there is no shortage of such creatures in a jungle!

During my tenure at Imphal as Commanding Officer of

No. 1 Squadron, I had another memorable experience. My Squadron was equipped with Hurricane aircraft. However, I was keen to fly a Spitfire which had earned even more fame in the Battle of Britain. The headquarters in the Imphal Valley had a Spitfire. After taking permission from the boss I did a couple of sorties locally. It was a very pleasant and more powerful aircraft to fly. The desire of most pilots is to fly higher and faster. To satisfy my ego further, I took it up for an operation over Burma. I saw a truck on a jungle road and started attacking it with cannon fire.

Immediately after the attack and during the process of levelling and pulling out, my engine fluttered and stopped. I was sweating with fright as the countryside down below was a thick and hostile jungle. In a frenzy, I moved my hands to many knobs which pilots are trained to check in such an emergency. When I moved the knob of the extra fuel tank the engine picked up just before the aircraft reached the stalling speed. It became normal within a few minutes. I still remember with awe my foolhardy act and the good luck I had on that day.

Lastly, I may mention just another incident. When the Imphal Valley was surrounded, our forces were expecting an attack for its capture at any time. I and another pilot were returning in a twin sortie over Burma about half an hour before sunset when I saw hordes of soldiers pouring down the slopes. They were undoubtedly the attacking Japanese forces making a dash for taking up positions for a night attack. Later we learnt that their objective was the Corps Headquarters. I informed the control about this force and they ordered every aircraft of No. 1 Squadron to take off and attack. By sunset all our aircraft, sixteen in number, were attacking the invaders.

We later learnt that the invaders turned back after heavy

casualties and, thereafter, no such daring attack was launched on the Valley. This action of No. 1 Squadron, in my opinion, saved the Imphal Valley from capture by the Japanese and, being a part of the Squadron, I always look back on it with nostalgia and satisfaction.

WAR

War is a monstrous atrocity against humanity. When you are in one, your intense concern is your own misery and deep terror. To survive you learn to cope. In the immediacy of terror you have to learn.

Arnold Benson

B-26, Bomber Pilot

Aye, Fight!, but not your neighbour. Fight rather all the things that cause you and your neighbour to fight.

Mikhail Naim

7

HIS CANDID VIEWS

Role of the Air Force has greatly enhanced as we can see from the US Campaign in Afghanistan, where the ground fighting has been minimized. So, it is crucial to recognize that the Air Force will play a primary role in any future war. We have to accept certain mishaps in the Air Force because flying involves human beings and there is always scope for wrong human judgment. In every case it could have been the error of the pilot or the equipment, I feel that if the pilots had proper training, it would have certainly made a difference.

- About operation Grand Slam, Indo-Pak Conflict of 1965, he says, "I am not a war monger, but I feel that if we had some more time, we would have done even better, however, we Indians are a very resilient race and our morale is always very high."
- On Diplomacy, he says, "There should be efforts made on all fronts including diplomacy. But I must commend the government for digging their heels on the issue of cross border terrorism with Pakistan."
- If he was the Air Chief today: he gives his evergreen and winsome smile and says, "The IAF is much more

technologically advanced than it ever was before. And the present Air Chief knows much more than what we did at our time. We were also modern, but not to such an extent."

- Advice is the biggest vice, and accordingly he says with all the humility, "I advise only when asked."
- On receiving the letter from the Defence Minister, George Fernandes at about 7 pm, he says, "It appears to have been written by the minister himself. The news has come as a complete surprise to me. But it is something I will value throughout life. The IAF had been talking about it for sometime now, but I was not really expecting it. But the decision only goes to show the importance the Government gives its Armed Forces. I think it is a good sign and I hope it continues to be like this."
- On the security situation and the Government actions subsequent to the attack on the Parliament House on December 13, 2001, he said the Government's timing in dealing with the situation had been proper.
- Humble as ever, he said, naturally I am immensely pleased, but an individual is nobody without the backing of the Service. An individual is judged by the performance of his organisation.
- He became the Chief of the IAF at the age of 44 in 1964, and retired from IAF in 1969 at the age of 50. "I served two tenures as the Chief of the IAF. After that I had no other option but to resign. I wanted to make way for new people to come up."
- Our Air Force is one of the most professional and finest fighting forces. My continued involvement with IAF gave me a sense of pride and fulfillment. IAF had given me a lot and now to be honoured as the first Marshal has ensured that I would never be dissociated from my parent organisation.

8

WOULD YOU DO IT AGAIN?

"The Air Force is My Life. Yes; I Would"

Sometime back, in an interview with *Times of India*, Marshal Arjan Singh had shared some of his inner thoughts during those momentous days when he was in the thick of it all:

It was kind of peculiar. The Quit India Movement was on and yet there were two million Indians fighting to maintain the British Empire. It's not that we were politically ignorant. We definitely had our sympathy with the freedom fighters. In our own way we were fighting for freedom—as young people we wanted to prove to the British that we were as good, if not better than they were. In a way we hastened the independence process because the British realized they could never use the Armed Forces to suppress the freedom movement.

For the whole of 1944 we fought against the Japanese. I logged about 450 hours in about 300 sorties. No. 1 was one of the main Squadrons in Manipur when the Valley was surrounded by the Japanese and INA. We were the only one to remain throughout the campaign. Also, we were the only

Squadron with 100% serviceability record. Most of our operations were in support of the Army. We operated as far as Rangoon.

"Was he ever scared?"

Initially it was quite frightening. During my first sortie I was quite afraid. But after a few sorties, and after my aircraft had been hit by ground fire, I took it as a routine. Sometimes with all the engine noise I didn't even know I had been hit. Once I came back with 10 or 12 bullet holes and realized only when I was back on the ground.

"Does he ever wonder, given the modern technology, how the Hurricanes came through?"

It was a very safe aircraft. We had complete faith in it, It was made of fabric and the bullets just went through it. The plane was flying so slow, it didn't really matter. So many of us came back with bullet holes. It is different with modern day aircraft.

Casualties?

The thought goes down after you have done one or two sorties. Those were different days. We were young in a different frame of mind. We had no family commitments. The thought of getting shot down really didn't bother us. Most of our casualties were due to the ground fire. Only three of the twenty-one, who were with me when I took command, came through.

His Finest Hour?

I was returning from a sortie in Burma. I saw a big force of Japanese trying to breakthrough the hills into the valley. I landed and reported. All other Squadrons had packed up. With half an hour to go for the sunset No. 1 Squadron took off and beat the hell out of them. It was most satisfying. Later on I was told our operation was the one that has saved the valley.

What was it really like?

Oh, it was wonderful. We lived in these straw *bashas*. We played games whenever we had the time. We ate good food. Let me tell you, as Squadron Leader I saved much more than ever after. Everything was free. There was no expenditure. We lived free, the food was free.

Was it worth it?

In the end, war is never worth it.

Would you do it again?

The Air Force is my life. Yes. I would.

LIFE

The life of every man is a diary in which he means to write one story but writes another one, and his humblest hour is when he compares the volume as it is with what he vowed to make.

E. Stanley Jones

The greatest use of life is to spend it on something that will outlast it.

Graffiti

Life: If you know how to use it, it is long enough.

Seneca

A Fond Farewell by one of the MiG Squadrons

9

IAF TAKES-OFF WITH TIGERS: BEGINNING OF AN EXCITING ODYSSEY

The early history of No.1 Squadron is synonymous to the history of the Indian Air Force. The history of No.1 Squadron, Air Force is saga of glory and the lives of the architects of this history have unrivalled record of redoubtable courage and distinguished service. Through the years, legends have grown around the glorious exploits of this Squadron and the names of those pioneers who nurtured military aviation in this country with visions of a great and resplendent future for this new service. Amongst these early pioneers were HC Sircar, Subroto Mukerjee (later Air Marshal and the First Indian CAS), AB Awan, Bhupendra Singh and Amarjeet Singh. They were later joined by AM Engineer (later DFC, Air Marshal and the Chief of the Air Staff), KK Majumdar (later Wing Commander, DFC and Bar). Narendra, Prithipal Singh, 'Baba' Mehar Singh and SN Goyal. Flight Lieutenant CA Bouchier, DFC, an Officer of the Royal Air Force, was the first commanding officer of the Squadron. Over 26 years later in September, 1959, Air Vice Marshal Sir Cecil Bouchier was to say "The Indian Air Force is what it is today because of; the imagination, courage, loyalty and great quality of the first little pioneer band of Indian Officers and Airmen, for they were the salt of the earth... . They have built up a great fighting service and I am proud to have been associated with this wonderful achievement, if only for a little while... ."

The Early Years

The years 1933 to 1937 were basically the formative years for the Squadron when it trained in its primary role of Army Co-operation from Drigh Road, Peshawar, Chakala and Sialkot.

On April 1, 1936, 'B' Flight of the Squadron was formed with one Westland Wapiti aircraft.

Such a humble beginning gave little indication of the glorious days to come, except to those visionary pioneers.

The rigorous training was to pay handsome dividends in September 1937 when the Squadron was inducted into operations against hostile tribesmen in North West Frontier Province. Operating from Miranshah in North Waziristan with just four Wapiti aircraft of 'A' flight, the Squadron flew 1437 hours in less than three months.

Flying Officer AM Engineer was the first IAF officer to be 'Mentioned in Despatches' for gallantry during these operations.

Soon after, then Flying Officer Subroto Mukerjee was appointed Flight Commander of 'A' Flight.

By the time 'C' Flight was formed and the three flights came together for the first time in Ambala, all three flight commanders were Indian. These were Flying Officers Subroto Mukerjee, AM Engineer and KK Majumdar.

On the historic day of March 16, 1939, Flight Lieutenant

Subroto Mukerjee took over the command of the Squadron from Squadron Leader CH Smith, thus becoming the first Indian to command a flight, a Squadron, later a station and finally, of course the Indian Air Force itself.

The Tigers indeed gave invaluable experience to a fledgling Air Force and contributed towards its growth. In a way the Squadron literally provided the nucleus of the Indian Air Force, as also the Pakistan Air Force for that matter. Six of the eight Chief of Staff of the Indian Air Force served with No.1 Squadron sometime or the other and three of them commanded the Squadron.

A Date with Pathans

The courage and initiative of the Squadron pilots is perhaps evident from the legendary 'Baba' Mehar Singh's escape from the hostile tribesmen in the North West Frontier.

In 1937, he was attacking a force of tribesmen in a particularly wild valley near Shaider, a place which had not been visited by the Army since Lord Kitchener's expedition in 1890. During the attack the fuel tank of the Wapiti was hit by ground fire. Every second increased the risk of fire which could destroy the fragile Wapiti's fabric surface. 'Baba' Mehar Singh force-landed the aircraft in the difficult rocky terrain of the valley. Fortunately, the bombs on the aircraft did not explode and Baba and his air gunner could crawl out of the wreckage safely. Hereafter, Baba and his air gunner successfully evaded the tribesmen, beating them at their own game till darkness came to their rescue. As dawn broke, they reached a tiny army post. With his indomitable spirit, Baba not only rejoined the Squadron immediately but was also airborne the very next day.

A similar incident occurred with then flying officer Arjan Singh in a Hawker Audax aircraft. This time his gunner started running towards the hostile tribesmen to avoid the fire from the aircraft. A reverse case of 'from the fire into the frying pan' to twist an old proverb. Arjan Singh not only managed to get his gunner back but also successfully evaded the tribesmen.

An incident emphasizing the ingenuity of the Squadron pilots occurred on the 7th of August, 1940. 'B' Flight of the Squadron based at Miranshah was operating in the Daur Valley in support of the land forces in the face of intense hostile ground fire. While flying one such mission Squadron Leader Subroto Mukerjee observed one of the army pickets being overwhelmed by the hostiles. The besieged troops indicated their ammunition was nearly exhausted. Subroto Mukerjee instructed his gunner to remove ammunition from the Magazine of the rear cockpit-mounted Lewis machine gun. The ammunition was put in their socks and successfully dropped to the troops in a low pass despite concentrated firing on the aircraft by the hostiles. This ammunition helped the picket to hold out till another aircraft came and dropped 800 more rounds of ammunition and saved the situation. This was perhaps the beginning of air maintenance in a rather ingenuous form.

In June 1939, the Squadron was re-equipped with Hawker Hart aircraft with a few Hawker Audax aircraft on its inventory. During the initial period of the Second World War the Squadron continued its patrolling and Army cooperation duties on a relatively quiet frontier. In August, 1941, the Squadron was re-equipped with 12 Lysander aircraft financed as a gift from the citizens of Bombay. Since then the Squadron is considered to have been adopted by Bombay and known as the Bombay Squadron.

EXPERIENCE

Experience increases our wisdom but doesn't reduce our follies. ***Josh Billing***

Experience teaches us at the expense of our illusions. ***Epigram***

Experience is the name everyone gives to his mistakes. ***Oscar Wilde***

After a somersault always lands sunny side up.

Graffti

Skill to do comes from doing. ***Proverb***

No one knows what he can do until he tries.

Proverb

President Dr S Radhakrishnan and Air Chief Marshal (now Marshal) Arjan Singh at IAF Day Reception.

10

BURMESE EXPERIENCE

For Your Tomorrow We Gave Our Today

Does Garrison Hill, Kohima, strike a chord?

Any chord?

Few would remember that the serene, cloud kissed place which houses a carefully-kept and terraced War Cemetry dotted with trees and flowering plants, was the scene of one of the most fierce and bloody battles of World War II. It is better known as the place where the famous Battle-For-The-Tennis-Court was fought. It was the limit of the Japanese advance into Indian territory during the Second World War, and is the most well-known of the War Cemetries in the North-East.

There is a large cross towering over the cemetry in Kohima, Nagaland, with the inscription that reads:

"Here around the Tennis Court
Of the Deputy Commissioner
Lie men who fought
In The Battle of Kohima
In which, they and their comrades
Finally halted the Invasion of India

By the forces of Japan in April 1944."

A stirring testimony to the days when the Allied and the Japanese soldiers fought virtually hand-to-hand for a few metres of ground. On the tennis court outside the DC's bungalow, is the epitaph:

"When you go back home
Tell them of us and say
For your tomorrow
We gave our today."

Today, neat rows of memorial plaques in the cemetry are a testimony to the many lives that were lost in the battle. But those lives had not been lost in vain. The victory of the Allies in the Battle of Kohima proved to be the turning point of the war on the eastern front. From Kohima and the surrounding villages, then along the Kohima-Imphal Road, the Japanese were steadily driven back by the Allies. The tide had begun to turn.

□

Today, Kohima (a corruption of 'Kew-Hima', meaning people from the land where the Kew flower is found) is a bustling little township where the Garrison Hill continues to occupy the vantage position. The War Cemetry is a major attraction for the proud Nagas as well as others, and each of the 1287 headstones tell a different story. Similar stately cemetries of the Allied soldiers commemorating Hindus, Sikhs, Muslims, Buddhists and Christians are found in Guwahati, Imphal and Ledo near Digboi. Besides these, the North-East is dotted with scores of War Memorials.

Here is a typical epitaph on the Garrison Hill:

"To the world,
Our Tom was just a soldier,

To us,
He was the whole world." *Mom & Dad*

The Japanese Onslaught

The ruthless efficiency and the lightning speed which Japan had shown at Pearl Harbour, characterized all its early operations. Their moves were not for mere 'Flag Showing' but determined 'Winning Moves'.

The British Battleships 'Prince of Wales', and 'Repulse', had reached Singapore on December 2, 1941, to boost the morale of British Forces in the Far East. They were promptly and effortlessly sunk by the Japanese aircraft on December 9, 1941.

Thereafter, there was no stopping of the Japanese and their stunning conquests followed one after the other in quick succession—Malaya, Phillipines, Hong Kong, Singapore.

The British had all through believed that Japanese would stay neutral, and their compelling rationale for this assessment was because they (British) were completely unprepared for war in the Far East, and wanted it to be that way. The Japanese entry into the war had created awe and confusion in the British Government circles. It was therefore decided to fight a rear-guard action in Malaya and withdraw the Forces to form an effective defence of Singapore. It was decided to defend Singapore to the last man.

Once again the British planners had failed to appreciate that the Japanese were not working to a timetable drawn up by the British. When speed was of the essence, the troops withdrawn from the Middle East were packed in slow moving convoys to Singapore which had a sailing time of over a week. Instead of flying them by aircraft to Singapore they had crated them in wooden boxes to be ferried across the ocean to the fast developing battle area.

With these none-too-wise moves, the inevitable happened.

The Japanese overran Malaya and captured Singapore before the British could realise WHAT IS HAPPENING.

This had brought the war to Burma—the Courtyard of India, well before the British could get their bearings right.

□

After the fall of Burma, the Japanese had been the virtual masters of a vast area stretching from the jungle covered mountains of Northern and Western Burma where the British and Indian troops were in close contact with them, across the sea to Andaman and Nicobar Islands and the Great Dutch Dependencies of Sumatra and Java, and a string of lesser islands of New Guinea.

The Americans had established a Bomber Force in China which had to be fed and maintained through airlift from Assam over the Southern Spurs of Himalayas which they called 'The Hump'.

The campaign in Northern Burma had opened in December, 1943, with General Stiwell's Forces crossing the watershed from Ledo into jungles below the mountain ranges. In the South, British XVth Corps under General Christison began their advance down the Arakan Coast on January 19, 1944.

It was against this backdrop of Land Operations that the Indian Air Force was called upon firstly to carry out Tactical Reconnaissance in the Theatre of Operations, and secondly to render support to our Army in Action. The Tasks were undertaken by our Squadrons flying Hurricanes and Vultee Vengeance Dive Bombers, virtual discards from the RAF.

Just to give you an idea about the Japanese fabled fighting skills and resolve, let me share with you the Order of the Day issued by Lieutenant General Renu Mutaguchi, General Officer Commanding, 15th Japanese Army in Burma:

"If your hands are broken, fight with your feet
If your feet are broken, fight with your teeth
If there is no breath left in your body
Fight with your ghost.
Lack of weapons is no excuse for defeat."

And the Japanese General meant every word of it.

What is important and noteworthy is that the Japanese soldiers willingly did precisely that.

The fighting qualities of the Japanese were aptly summed up by Field Marshal Viscount Slim, who said:

"We all talk a lot about fighting to the last man and the last round, but the Japanese soldier is the only one who actually does it."

They were indeed a worthy enemy.

□

Sir Winston Churchill while fighting a World War, was far too occupied with the problems at home and had spelt out his War Priorities in 1941, as under:

"First, the defence of the island including the threat of invasion, and U-boat war. Secondly, the struggle in the Middle East and the Mediterranean. Thirdly, after June, supplies to Soviet Russia, and last of all, resistance to Japanese Assault."

It was, however, understood that if Japan invaded Australia and New Zealand, the Middle East should be sacrificed to the defence of 'our kith and kin'.

□

The First Burma Campaign

No. 1 Squadron, led by Sqn Ldr 'Jumbo' Majumdar started its move to the east, reaching Toungoo in Burma on 1st February 1942, and prepared to face the mighty Japanese forces with their handful of Lysanders, along with those of No. 28 Squadron, RAF. On the very first night itself, the Japanese Air Force raided Toungoo and Jumbo decided to reciprocate the very next day. Although meant only for tactical reconnaissance, No. 1 Squadron's personnel fixed pairs of 250 lb bombs on the Lysander wheel spats and No. 1 Squadron launched raids against the Japanese airfields at Mae-Haugsuan, Cheingmai and Chiangrai in Siam, missions flown at low level without escort and evoking great praise from the American Volunteer Group (AVG) and New Zealander pilots.

On February 5, 1942, No.1 Squadron was moved to Mingaladon, just outside Rangoon and the next day, Jumbo led Nos.1 and 28 Squadrons on a combined raid against Japanese-held dockyards and the railway junction at Moulmein. The ground troops were heartened by the display of Lysanders in flight echelon formation, staggering along with their bomb loads and direct hits were scored on the targets, the dockyard erupting in flames which could be seen from 60 miles away. The Lysanders flew back at almost ground level over the Martaban and General Wavell, the Commander-in-Chief, sent a personal signal congratulating Majumdar and the two Squadrons.

Mingaladon was frequently raided by the Japanese Air Force. The American Volunteer Group P 40s used to be quick off the ground to engage the raiders and many furious dog fights were witnessed. At night, the allied fighters were dispersed to a number of satellite airstrips, two nicknamed

Johnny Walker and John Haig after the famous brands of Scotch whisky! On February 18, the RAF and AVG tore into 40 Japanese bombers and shot down 12 of them.

From Mingaladon, No.1 Squadron essentially carried out tactical and photo reconnaissance and operated important staff communication flights. During the second week of February, the Squadron was split, as the Chinese 5th Army in northern Burma urgently needed reconnaissance aircraft for army cooperation.

Sqn Ldr Majumdar and Flt Lt Prithipal Singh took several pilots and Lysanders north to Lashio, Flt Lt Prasad remained at Mingaladon with his flight while Flt Lt Raza went to Toungoo with his flight to carry out tactical recce. Thereafter, the various detachments were cut off from each other as the Japanese advanced and as communications steadily worsened, pilots and air gunners often improvised maintenance on their own. At Mingaladon, Flt Lt Prasad and his flight were busy bombing in the Pegu area and along the Siam border. The main body of No.1 Squadron kept the Japanese airstrip near Ywathit in Siam under check and to convince the doubting Chinese of the imminent danger, Sqn Ldr Majumdar had to once actually do a 'touch and go' with his Lysander on the enemy airstrip!

Throughout the second half of February, Flt Lt Raza operated his sole Lysander from Toungoo, which was raided every day by the Japanese. Raza carried out daily recce of all approaches from the Sittang river along the Siam borders.

The Japanese hit Toungoo with ten bombers on 27th February, escorted by nine fighters but the next evening, Raza hit back at the Japanese airfield at Mehongson, strafing the enemy aircraft at dispersal and bombing the wireless cabin.

On the 1st March, Raza flew the last Lysander out to Lashio, with Sgt Cabinetmaker (the technician) driving away a steam engine loaded with refugees, the last one out of Toungoo before the Japanese occupation.

At Lashio, on 7th March, Flt Lt Raza and Rajinder Singh flew RAF pilots in their Lysanders to Mingaladon to recover two abandoned Hurricanes and all four aircrafts, then flew back to Magwe. For five days (7-11 March) the last six Lysanders of No.1 Squadron carried out continuous patrol over General Alexander's Army as they retreated from Burma. On March 12, the Lysanders were handed over to the Burmese Communication Flight and No.1 Squadron's pilots flew back to India in a USAAF Flying Fortress.

For his exceptional courage, leadership and fighting spirit, Sqn Ldr KK Majumdar was awarded the DFC, the first Indian to be so honoured, while Warrant Officer Harjinder Singh was awarded the MBE for his imaginative improvisation and keeping the Squadron at high serviceability in almost impossible conditions.

Marshal Leads the Tiger

After withdrawal from Burma, No. 1 Squadron re-assembled at Secundrabad, once more under the command of Sqn Ldr S Mukerjee, and then moved to Trichinopoly in May. In June, 14 pilots and 45 NCOs proceeded to No. 151 Operational Training Unit at Risalpur for conversion to the Hurricane IIB fighter, collecting their allotted aircraft at the Drigh Road Depot and then, under brief command of Sqn Ldr Henry Runganadhan, went back to Trichinopoly. In October 1942, the Squadron's Crest was officially approved, being a full Tiger profile enclosed in two concentric circles, officially approved, with the motto *Ittehad Main Shakti Hai*,

later modified to *Ekta Main Shakti* (or 'in unity there is strength'). Henry was succeeded by Sqn Ldr SN Goyal and the Squadron changed its location several times in the next year, being moved to Bairagarh then Chhara, and back to Risalpur. In May, a detachment went to Miranshah for bombing trials and then the Tigers moved to Kohat where command was assumed by Sqn Ldr Arjan Singh on September 3, 1943. During the next few months, No. 1 Squadron detachments moved to Miranshah and carried out army cooperation exercises at Adampur, in Punjab.

In early December 1943, Field Marshal Sir Claude Auchinleck visited the RAF Station at Kohat and inspected No.1 Squadron. Sqn Ldr Arjan Singh advocated the intense desire of No.1 Squadron to go back into battle. This was supported by the RAF Station Commander. Within a week of this request, No.1 Squadron (now with Hurricane IIBs) was ordered to move immediately to Imphal on the Manipur front where massive buildups were taking place on both sides of the Assam-Burma border. The next year was to be breathless with action in the history of the Tiger Squadron.

Guts-N-Glory

No.1 Squadron reached Imphal (Main) on February 3, 1944, and were to remain in action for a record period of 14 months, taking vital part in the fateful siege of Imphal followed by the trans-Chindwin and trans-lrrawaddy offenses. Once again, No.1 Squadron IAF shared the base with their old collegues-in-arms No. 28 Squadron RAF, both being Tactical Reconnaissance Units (Tac/R), co-operating closely with the Army.

The Tigers under Sqn Ldr Arjan Singh commenced operational flying immediately, with sector reconnaissances flown on February 5, carrying out offensive, tactical and photographic reconnaissances to observe Japanese movements on the Chindwin, beyond Tiddim, and as far east as the Myitkyina-Mandalay railway, much valuable information being obtained by the Squadron.

The Japanese offensive against Imphal started on March 8, attempting to cut off the 17th Indian Division as it retreated. No.1 Squadron's task was to locate the position of the retreating troops day to day and to keep the tracks leading from the Tiddim Road under observation for Japanese movements. On March 29, during a late evening reconnaissance flown by the CO, Japanese troops were seen clambering down the hills. Landing back at Imphal Main to refuel, the entire Squadron was led back by Arjan Singh into the area before sunset and the Hurricanes hammered the enemy with machine guns and bombs, decimating the Japanese advance battalion, with 14 officers and 217 men killed or wounded.

During March, the Squadron had flown 366 sorties and no Japanese fighters were encountered yet but April 1944 was to be a crucial month when the siege of Imphal tightened and the Japanese came so close that the Imphal airfields were within range of enemy artillery fire. Maximum air effort was put in by No.1 Squadron, flying 412 sorties in April, tactical reconnaissance mostly over the Tiddim Road, Palel-Tamu-Sittaung road, Imphal-Kohima road and the Ukhrul road. The Tigers strafed *bashas*, mechanical transport, gun positions and troops. In turn, Japanese Kawasaki Ki48 and Mitsubishi Ki21 bombers raided Imphal on April 15, damaging two of No.1 Squadron's Hurricanes.

During May 1944, the weather deteriorated with early

Aerodromes in Burma February-March 1942

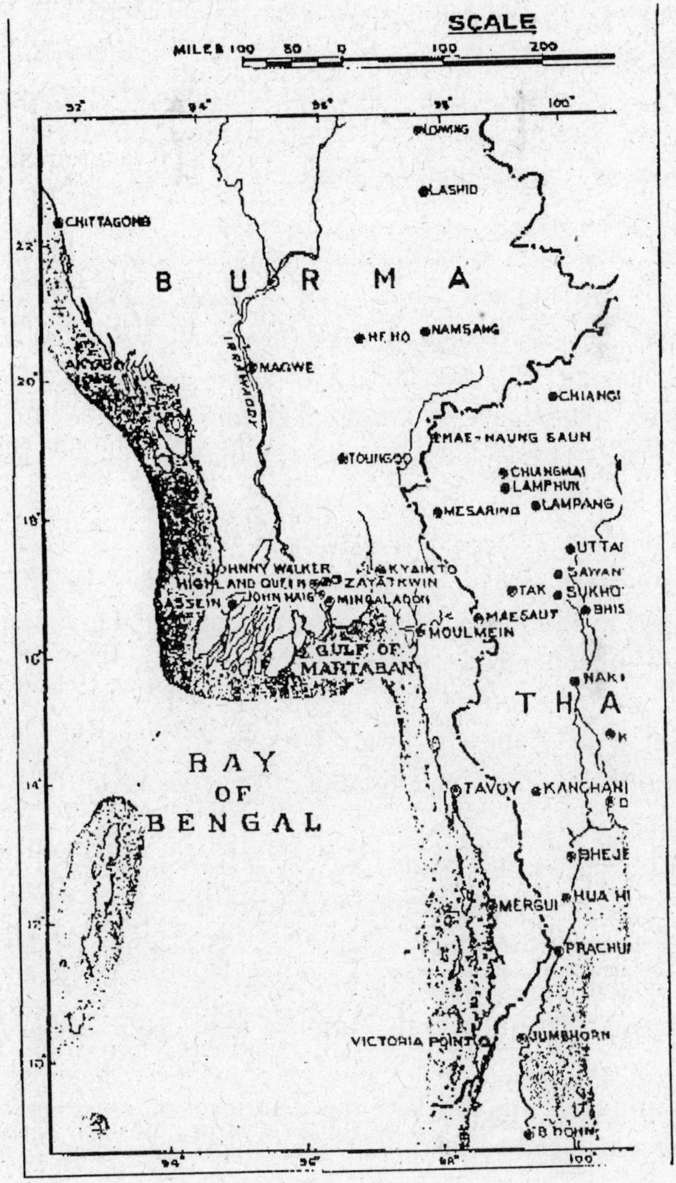

SCALE
MILES 100 50 0 100 200

BURMA
THA
BAY OF BENGAL
GULF OF MARTABAN
IRRAWADDY

LOWING
LASHIO
CHITTAGONG
HEHO
NAMSANG
MAGWE
CHIANG
MAE-HAUNG SAUN
TOUNGOO
CHIANGMAI
LAMPHUN
MESARING
LAMPANG
UTTA
SAWAN
JOHNNY WALKER
KYAIKTO
HIGHLAND QUEEN
ZAYATKWIN
JOHN HAIG
MINGALADON
TAK
SUKHO
BHIS
MAESAUT
MOULMEIN
NAK
TAVOY
KANCHAN
BHEJE
MERGUI
HUA HI
PRACHU
VICTORIA POINT
JUMBHORN

monsoon rains which curtailed flying, yet No.1 Squadron flew 372 sorties, including 32 by night, that month, which also had the loss of a long range reconnaissance Hurricane to prowling Japanese Nakajima Ki 43 ('Oscar') fighters. No.1 Squadron's aircraft ranged over almost the entire battlefield, carrying out continuous tactical reconnaissance as in the area north-east of Imphal the Japanese were being gradually pushed back.

June 1944 was an even more trying month, with the runways waterlogged while rain storms made flying hazardous. No. 28 Squadron RAF had been pulled out of Imphal, leaving No.1 Squadron IAF solely responsible for tactical reconnaissance in the area, flying 327 sorties that month. The Tiger's Hurricane IIBs (with machine guns) were replaced by Hurricane IICs (with cannon), for greater effect in ground attack missions. The siege of Imphal was broken by the month-end and the Squadron was tasked to keep harassing the retreating Japanese, mainly in the Ukhrul area and south of Imphal. Reconnaissance was carried out over the roads and tracks from Palel to Sittaung on the Chindwin, from Tamu to Kamjong, from Htinzin to Yazagyo, the Chindwin river and so on, a total of 307 sorties being flown in July.

During the ensuing battle for Central Burma, the British-Indian forces mounted relentless pressure on the retreating Japanese beyond the Chindwin and No.1 Squadron, as part of the 221 Group, operated from forward bases covering a front of some 200 miles to the limits of their endurance and range. In August, No.1 Squadron flew 354 sorties, with targets of opportunity being attacked, but deteriorating weather in September reduced sorties to 292, but these were longer in duration, and the Hurricanes fitted with extra fuel tanks. On September 17, the Tigers attacked bunkers on a hill feature in the Yazagyo area and Taukkyan airfield south-west of Kalemyo. And so in October, with the Squadron flying a record 439 operational missions totalling 780 hours, the Tigers operating to as far as the Mandalay-Myitkyina railway. The value of No.1 Squadron's tactical reconnaissance was gratefully acknowledged by XXXIII Corps, and the Squadron was commended "for the skill and speed with which air photographs have been produced and dropped on forward troops."

One are Second to None

The Japanese continued to fall back and in November, No. 1 Squadron were discovering their lines of retreat. With an average strength of 17 pilots, the Tigers flew 524 operational sorties, totalling just over 1000 flying hours, a most remarkable effort! On the night of November 3, Arjan Singh had carried out a vital low level tac/recce of the bridge at Hpaungzeik, enabling the allies to move across and No. 1 Squadron received a notable appreciation of its efforts from GOC 20th Indian Division who presented them with a Japanese Sword of Honour captured in the battle of Imphal in recognition of 'assistance readily and courageously given by its pilots and ground crews'. Reinforced by their old collegues from No. 28 Squadron RAF, the Tigers flew 335 sorties for the XIV Army in December 1944, which saw beginning of the trans-Chindwin offensive.

In January 1945, now under command of Sqn Ldr Raja Ram, and given the task of tac/recce for IV Corps which had been secretly moved to the south for the advance towards the Irrawaddy and the strategic airfield and communication centre of Meiktila, No.1 Squadron moved from Imphal to an airstrip at Kan, north of Gangaw and the Tigers entered a new phase of intensive activity. The Irrawaddy was crossed on February 14, 1945 and the Squadron covered the deception movements southwards, up to Sale, Mondaing and Tanaunggyin, north of the Myingan-Meiktila road. A detachment of No.1 Squadron was moved to Sinthe, north of Pyinchaung, to cover the Irrawaddy crossing and in two days, the detachment flew 60 sorties. As the offensive made progress, the Squadron also extended the area of its activity but intense Japanese Ack-Ack fire claimed four aircraft damaged and one shot down in February 1945.

Meiktila fell in March and fierce Japanese counter attacks were held with the aid of fighter-bombers. No.1 Squadron was constantly in the air and flew 618 hours in March 1945, inspite of the fact that nine aircraft had been damaged by a sneak Japanese air raid on the airfield early in the month. By the month-end, No. 1 Squadron started to shephard No. 7 Squadron into the Sinthe area, the 'Battle Axes' tasked to relieve the veteran 'Tigers' as the Japanese retreated further.

This brought to a close a fantastic operational tour of months in the course of which No. 1 Squadron flew 4813 operational sorties totalling 7220 hours. The value and reliability of the Squadron's vital work was recognized time and again and in his farewell message, the AOC 221 Group said, "the reliability of their Tac/R and photographic work has remained at a high level throughout and ground crews have set a record of serviceability of aircraft which is second to none in any Air Force in the World." No. 1 Squadron's Hurricanes were kept at a 99% serviceability, the highest in the 3rd Tactical Air Force. The Squadron Commander had

been awarded an immediate DFC in the field, Lord Louis Mountbatten pinning the coveted medal personally on Sqn Ldr Arjan Singh and on completion of its operational tour, another 6 DFCs were awarded to No. 1 Squadron, plus innumerable other awards including that to the SEO, Flt Lt Ram Singh.

No. 1 Squadron of the now Royal Indian Air Force returned to India and were posted back to Kohat in April-May 1945 from where they had set out for war in late 1943. Still flying the sturdy Hurricane IIBs, No.1 Squadron's reins were handed over to Sqn Ldr E Nazirullah in August 1945 and the Tigers started to convert to the Spitfire VIII later in the year. Young Flying Officer Dilbagh Singh had joined No. 1 Squadron in May at Kohat and also converted to Spitfires in December 1945. While with the detachment at Miranshah, he flew an operational sortie on February 1946, responding to a 'XX call' from the Tochi Scouts, making three cannon firing passes against hostile tribesmen in Sangar for which he was given an immediate commendation.

In March 1946, Sqn Ldr Ranjan Dutt took over as CO of No. 1 Squadron which, in April 1946, moved to Samungli (Quetta) via Fort Sandeman. After flying in the Baluchistan area for some months, No. 1 Squadron RIAF moved with its Spitfire VIIIs to southern India, being located at Yelahanka, near Bangalore in August 1946. In September, the Squadron took part in a series of flypasts, marking the anniversary of victory over Japan but the Tiger's forte remained close air support, training with the army in the Kolar-Bangalore-Bombay area. Operating from Santa Cruz (Bombay) in December 1946, the Squadron's Spitfires took part in a combined-services demonstration and in the early months of

1947, flew sorties ranging from St.Thomas Mount (Madras) to Poona to Madh Island to Hakimpet and back to base at Yelahanka. Some Griffon-engined spitfires XIVs were received in March 1947 but the decision had been taken for No. 1 Squadron to convert to the more powerful Centaurus-powered Hawker Tempest II.

Conversion on the Tempest II began in May 1947 at Risalpur, the Squadron rapidly becoming fully operational on the new type and by July, having moved to Peshawar, detachments took part in operations against the *Faqir* of Ipi's tribesmen in the NWFP.

WAR

War is province of physical exertion and suffering.

Carl Van Clauswitz

War is nothing but a duel on a large scale.

Carl Von Clanswitz

There is no such thing as an inevitable war. If war comes it will be from failure of human wisdom.

Bonar Law

War bring scars.

English Proverb

Wars are pleasant to the ears, not the eyes.

Horace

11

TIGERS AFTER 1947

Tigers into Hibernation

As the countdown to Independence—and partition—of the country began in mid-1947, division of the Armed Forces became a painful reality. While the assets of the Royal Indian Air Force were to be divided as per the determined formula, the personnel were given little choice: Muslims were to be transferred to Pakistan, others to remain with the RIAF. Most of the permanent airbases (barring Ambala), plus training and infrastructural facilities were geographically situated in what was to be a new (and very rapidly, hostile) country.

An Air Force Reconstitution Committee, under the chairman-ship of Air Vice Marshal Allan Perry-Keene (soon appointed as C-in-C of the Royal Pakistan Air Force), reconsidered the original allotments (Nos. 6 and 9 Squadrons for the RPAF) and increased the fighter allocation by another Squadron. Shockingly, No.1 Squadron, the very foundation of the India's air arm, was designated as the other fighter unit for Pakistan and this act of infamy has never been seriously debated or explained by those in power at the time.

Till April 1947, No.1 Squadron was operating Spitfire

VIIIs from Yelahanka under the command of Sqn Ldr Ranjan Dutt who had taken over as CO in March 1946. In May 1947, the Tigers moved north, to Peshawar for conversion onto the Tempest II and by July were in action with their new fighters against dissident tribesmen in the NWFP. On July 7 and 8, 1947, for example, Fg Offr Lakshman Katre flying Tempest (PR 796) dropped warning leaflets over Swabi, Kalukhan and a few days later, over Kharak and Bannu.

However, the die had been cast and Katre's last sortie on a No. 1 Squadron Tempest was on July 25 when PR 718 and PR 600 were ferried from Peshawar to Miranshah and Miranshah to Risalpur. The trauma of partition was upon No.1 Squadron, the country ravaged by communal frenzy and the Tigers were directly affected. All Tempests and supporting equipment were officially alloted to the newly formed Royal Pakistan Air Force at the midnight of August 14-15 and young Fg Offr Katre with non-Muslim ground personnel of No.1 Squadron departed Peshawar by special train for the eastern part of partitioned Punjab, leaving behind the beloved Tiger Squadron at Peshawar.

But what really transpired on August 15, 1947 at Peshawar was to become known much later. The RPAF recieved 24 Tempest IIs as its share plus some Dakotas and Austers. When the RPAF officially came into being on August 15, 1947, the Tempests were allocated to Nos. 9 and 5 Squadrons, RPAF, the former continuing its lineage from No. 9 Squadron RIAF but the latter, formed that very hour, had most of its (Muslim) personnel and all its flying and ground assets from No.1 Squadron RIAF! The curious implication was that the newly found country wanted as little to do with its previous (unpartitioned) roots even though No.1

Squadron had been formed at Drigh Road near Karachi, now capital of Pakistan and had cut its teeth in the North West Frontier (again now part of Pakistan).

Even more curious was the attempt to link No. 5 Squadron RPAF with No. 5 Squadron of the Royal Air Force (nee Royal Flying Corps). In the official PAF history, July 15, 1948 is shown as the 'first anniversary of No. 5 Squadron as a RPAF unit, the original having been established in 1913!'

So, in fact, although No. 1 Squadron RIAF was officially allocated to Pakistan, it actually disappeared or went into oblivion on the midnight of August 14, 1947, and the Pakistan Air Force have never since raised a No.1 Squadron as an operational formation (there is now a recently established No. 1 Flying Training Unit). Thus, the Tigers can be considered as having gone into hibernation. to be awoken or aroused or 'resuscitated' on February 1, 1953, some five and a half years later, as the No. 1 Squadron of the Indian Air Force at Halwara in Punjab.

Tigers Leap Back

India nearly went to war with Pakistan in 1950 and again in 1951, with Pakistan's Prime Minister Liaquat Ali Khan shaking his 'Nailed Fist' against India. In 1950 the Indian Air Force still had just five fighter/Squadrons, all flying Tempest IIs, with a handful of Vampires in a testing unit. The spectre of war against the neighbour which had just re-equipped its three lighter Squadrons with the more advanced Hawker Fury, and had ordered jet fighters (Supermarine Attacker) for a fourth, was distinctly uncomfortable and the lAF's fighter force was to be augmented by three new Squadrons, albeit equipped with obsolete Spitfire XVIIIs, some fifty of which were held in reserve stocks. Thus No. 2

Squadron (number plated in 1948) was resurrected, and two new units (Nos.14 and 15 Squadrons) raised, all equipped with the Spitfire XVIII at Ambala. Two disused airfields in the Punjab, near Jullunder and Ludhiana (Adampur and Halwara respectively) were reactivated in 1951.

No. 15 Squadron, commanded by Sqn Ldr E Dhatigara, was based at Halwara and did particularly well in armament work, air-to-ground gunnery and rocket attacks at various courses, winning the prestigious distinction at Jamnagar. On their return to Halwara, No. 15 were visited by Air Commodore Arjan Singh, Commanding No. 1 Operational Group in Delhi and this personal inspection confirmed that the Squadron was worthy of a unique distinction which was unknown to any but the select few at Air Headquarters. No. 1 Squadron, the old Tigers were to be 'resuscitated' and No. 15 Squadron was to provide personnel and aircraft for the purpose. Thus, on January 26, 1953, the Tigers of No. 1 Squadron were back in form and substance while No. 15 was number plated.

The Tigers did some shake down flights on the venerable Spitfire XVIIIs but only a few days later, in the first days of February 1953, the first four Vampire FB 52 jet fighter bombers were received (IB 203, IB 209, IB 345, HB 765). The air station Halwara was spartan in terms of buildings or hangers, so the aircraft were parked on the tarmac or in open pens, the officers and men accommodated in dug-in tents. Flt Lt CV 'Chandu' Gole was posted in as adjutant.

Flying conversion training began with instructors from No. 8 Squadron (already on Vampires) and the Tigers were quickly operational in record time. By August 1953, No. 1 Squadron had reached its full unit establishment of 16

Vampire FB 52s. The Tigers took part in both air defence as well as army support exercises and inspite of the difficult 'field conditions', in scorching heat or heavy monsoon rains, the Squadron maintained very high serviceability, thanks to the efforts of 'Chiefy' Flight Sergeant Karam Singh and his airmen. In September 1953, No. 1 Squadron moved from Halwara to Palam (Delhi) and to what was, in comparison, 'luxurious' facilities for the personnel as well as aircraft. With the move came a change in command, with Sqn Ldr TS 'Timki' Brar taking over No. 1 Squadron on September 25, 1953. 'Timki' was to command the Tigers for the next 30 months. No. 1 Squadron was now based at the capital and a grand reunion dinner was held in the Delhi Gymkhana Club, attended by Tigers, past and present. There were Sardar Surjit Singh Majithia (later Dy Minister for Defence), Roop Chand (later Ambassador), Subroto Mukerjee (later first Indian to be Air Chief), Aspy Engineer, Arjan Singh, RHD Singh, Nanda, Harjinder Singh, Nifty Pandit and others, including the young Pilot Officers of No. 1 Squadron. An earlier reunion, in 1949, had had some RPAF officers, including Asghar Khan came to Delhi for the occasion, even though the Tigers were in hibernation at the time.

Over the next three years, No.1 Squadron remained at Palam, apart from the routine moves to Jamnagar (or its satellite airfield Khambalia) for armament training and firing exercises. On April 3, 1956, Sqn Ldr GD 'Nobby' Clarke took over reins of the Tigers, the Squadron continuing at Palam with the Vampire FB 52 till it was to undergo yet another transformation, a metaphysical move, east to the new air base at Kalaikunda, south-east of Kolkata and equipped with the brand new French-origin transonic Mystere IVA, under the leadership of Sqn Ldr Dilbagh Singh on February 15, 1957. On the same date, at Palam, Sqn Ldr Clarke found himself designated as CO of the brand new No. 27 Squadron, equipped with Vampire FB 52s.

First on Mysteres

In the mid-fifties, the Government of India was seized with the urgent need to acquire contemporary jet fighters to counter build up of the Pakistan Air Force which was receiving Sabre jet fighters under US military aid. A number of options were examined and, in 1956, a contract was formalized with France for the supply of Dassault Mystere IVA jet fighters. These were to be the first swept wing, transonic fighters with the Indian Air Force and specially selected pilots and technical personnel were sent for conversion training to France. Led by Sqn Ldr Dilbagh Singh who had just returned to India after a fighter leader's course in the UK, ten experienced fighter pilots, with above average ratings, arrived in France on October 5, 1956, and were attached to the French Air Force's 2nd Squadron/2nd Wing at Dijon on the Cote d'Or. Operational conversion training was imparted on Mystere IVs which continued till February 1957, and on February 14, Dilbagh Singh was formally designated Commanding Officer of No.1 Squadron, the first IAF unit to be equipped with the Mystere IVA.

The bulk of aircraft were delivered to India by sea (on board a French Navy carrier) and acceptance tests were carried out at Santa Cruz airport (Bombay) in early May 1957. On May 17, *en route* to eastern India, Mysteres were inspected by India's Prime Minister Jawaharlal Nehru at Palam and the first 'official' supersonic bang over India was demonstrated by Dilbagh in a Mystere (IA 950) on May 17.

The Tigers reassembled at Kalaikunda in May 1957, under command of Dilbagh Singh with Omi Taneja as senior Flight Commander to work out fighter combat tactics and other standard procedures. Omi soon moved across the tarmac to oversee conversion of No. 8 Squadron also onto Mysteres and by 1959, all three designated Squadrons (Nos. 1, 3 and 8) had been equipped and Kalaikunda became an all-Mystere base.

Two years later, in December 1961, the Tigers were operationally deployed for the first time with their Mysteres when, under command of Sqn Ldr S Bhattacharya, they took part in 'Operation Vijay', the police action to oust the Portuguese from their colonies of Goa, Daman and Diu. No.1 Squadron operated from Santa Cruz for the air defence of Bombay and a 4-aircraft mission struck against Portuguese defences in Daman, firing T10 rockets, dropping bombs and hastening surrender of the garrison.

In October 1962, the Tigers moved from Kalaikunda to Halwara, their first airbase in Punjab, just about the time of the treacherous attack by Chinese forces against Indian defences in the north and north-east. The Tigers were on full alert and ready to go into action but the powers-that-were chose not to deploy air power. A year later, in September 1963, No.1 Squadron moved to Adampur near Jullunder and thus began what was to be the longest stay at a permanent location in the history of the Tigers—some 17½ years! A year later, on September 14, 1964, Omi Taneja took command of No. 1 Squadron and he was destined to lead the Tigers in full-scale war just a year later.

Tigers at War: September 1965

War clouds had gathered over the subcontinent in April

1965, initially at the unlikely corner of the Rann of Kutch and the possibility of battle inspired the Tigers (and the rest of the IAF) into improving serviceability of aircraft, camouflage on ground, passive air defences and, of course, operational flying aspects. War-like events in Kashmir from early August resulted in more intense activity and preparations for action, with armed dawn and dusk patrols flown, most pilots becoming fully operational. And additional pilots were attached to the Squadron, which was led by Omi Taneja, with Paddy, Earle and S Handa as Flight Commanders. When full scale war broke out on September 6, 1965, the Tigers were unleashed, the very first four Mystere armed reconnaissance being led by the CO. In the Gujranwala and Wazirabad sectors, with rolling stock transporting POL struck at Chakker railway station.

September 7, 1965 was a red letter day for No.1 Squadron who were given the honour to lead the attack against the PAF's main fighter base at Sargodha, a tactical target of major importance and housing nearly half of the enemy's combat force, and having formidable air defences. The entire Squadron was to take part but even as air crew reported for briefing at 0415 hours, Adampur was raided by PAF B-57 bombers. Notwithstanding, all pilots were strapped in their Mysteres by 0510 after the briefing: it was to be a 12 aircraft strike, in three sections of four, with two aircraft as standby. The Mysteres took off in pairs and proceeded towards Sargodha at deck level in the semi-darkness, observing total R/T silence, arriving with perfect navigation over the target just as dawn was breaking at 0550 hrs. Omi broke silence as Red Section pulled up for attack from 50 feet, firing rockets into an aircraft hanger, and then against a 4-engined transport aircraft. Blue Section, following, fired rockets against the PAF fighters at the ORP. Even as they exited, PAF F-104 Starfighters and F-86 Sabres on combat air patrol attempted to intercept the Mysteres but all, except one, returned safely to base. The sole loss was Sqn Ldr Tubby Devayya, on attachment with No. 1 Squadron, whose Mystere was presumably shot down by a Sidewinder missile but not before this doughty flyer from Coorg had first hit and destroyed a supersonic Starfighter. (This amazing feat was recognized only two decades later and Devayya posthumously awarded the MVC.) White Section meanwhile had had to return to base because of poor visibility and light conditions, but after refuelling, flew back to attack Sargodha with bombs in broad daylight, this audacious action catching the PAF unawares at 1000 hrs, destroying more F-86s on the ground. The last strike of the day was carried out by two Mysteres in the afternoon, but one aircraft was lost to enemy action.

Hereafter, No. 1 Squadron's Mysteres were tasked for close air support in the Chhamb and Sialkot sectors. The Squadron was visited by that great Tiger leader, Air Marshal Arjan Singh now Chief of the Air Staff. The Tigers continued their forays into West Pakistan, attacking targets of opportunity, lending close air support to the Army despite intense ground fire and intercepting PAF Sabres. Even as PAF B-57s continued their nocturnal raids on Adampur, No.1 Squadron countered with interdiction sorties by day, destroying armoured fighting vehicles and continuing with close air support missions for the Army. Because of the nuisance of night air raids, the Squadron was continuously re-deployed, to Ambala or even Palam. Mystere strikes against enemy armour in the Chawinda-Pasrur sector were covered by Gnat escorts and Sabres were kept off the Tigers' backs. The last sortie of the war was once more led by the CO before the ceasefire took effect on September 23.

The Tigers had flown 174 operational sorties, serviceability had remained very high, two aircraft and their pilots had been lost to enemy action but the Tigers had taken their toll—two F-86s, one C-130, one F-104 destroyed plus many aircraft damaged, 12 tanks, numerous 'B' vehicles, 2 bridges, rail tankers and gun positions destroyed. Even as the Squadron 'stood down' 30 ops u/t pilots were converted to fully ops status, with over 800 hours flown without incident just after the ceasefire. No. 1 Squadron personnel were awarded three Vir Chakras, plus numerous VMs, VSMs and mention-in-despatches.

Tigers Go Bisonic

The Tigers remained at Adampur with their Mysteres through the winter of 1965-66, even as relationships between the warring neighbours slowly returned to some normalcy. In mid-1966, the Squadron prepared for re-equipment with the Bisonic MiG-21 fighter. As per the unique decision, No. 1 Squadron was the only formation to convert to this new generation fighter as a complete unit, unlike other cases when pilots and technicians were handpicked from various Squadrons. The last Mystere sortie by the Tigers was flown in June 1966 and from July, flying conversion training began on the new type at Adampur itself. The first four MiG-21 FLs (Type 77 in IAF nomenclature) allotted was augmented by the remaining aircraft in August-September 1966 and No. 1 Squadron was declared fully operational on their new Bisonic mount within a few months. Wg Cdr Omi Taneja had the singular distinction of being with the Tigers when they got the first Mysteres in 1956-57 and now, ten years later, was to lead them with the new aircraft for another year till September, 1967.

Thirty-five years after their establishment and after numerous police actions, a World War and some other operational tenures, the Tigers were presented the President's Colours. Now under command of Wg Cdr BN Misra, No. 1 Squadron, appropriately, became the first Indian Air Force formation to be given their Standard, presented by President Zakir Hussain at Adampur air base on October 18, 1968.

On September 28, 1970, Wg Cdr Upkar Singh took over command of No. 1 Squadron and his tenure of some three years, about the same length as Omi Taneja's was to be equally eventful both in terms of the length of time as also distinguished in action, for he was to lead the Tigers into war once more, in December 1971.

Operation Cactus Lily

The March 1971 showdown in the erstwhile East Pakistan spawned a chain of events that inevitably took India and Pakistan to armed conflict once again. For months Pakistan's armed forces mounted severe retribution on rebellious East Bengalis leading to millions seeking refuge in India. Apart from the immense economic burden and human tragedy, there were also security aspects and the danger of insurgency spilling into eastern India. Countdown to war began in the summer of 1971 and sporadic border incidents along the West Bengal-East Pakistan frontiers escalated into regular fighting towards the year end. On December 3, 1971, in an act of desperation, the Pakistan Air Force launched pre-emptive strikes against eight IAF air bases in Punjab and Rajasthan and the phony war was now for real.

No. 1 Squadron with its MiG-21 FLs were in readiness at Adampur when the undeclared war on the western front began at 1740 hrs on December 3. Four PAF Mirage IIIs and two F-104s had struck at Amritsar's Rajasansi airport and the nearby radar station, with negligible damage. However, the Tigers were scrambled to intercept but the raiders had tailed it back. More PAF strikes were carried out against IAF air bases but from 2350 hrs the Indian Air Force retaliated in massive manner with raids on enemy air bases and strategic targets carried out all night. No. 1 Squadron's prime responsibility was air defence of Adampur and the north-western Punjab sector as also escort to the Su-7s (from Adampur) on strike missions.

Dawn and dusk combat air patrols were flown, the MiG-21s vectored to intercept incoming raids but the PAF did not attempt to attack Adampur. The Tigers provided CAPs over Amritsar, Pathankot and their own base and on December 5, four fighters led by Wg Cdr Upkar Singh carried out a medium-level sweep over Chander Rahwali and Gujranwala, but the PAF did not respond to the Tigers' challenge.

On the 6th evening, two MiG-21s escorted 4 Su-7s on a strike mission in the Sialkot sector but again, there was no engagement with the PAF. On the 7th, the MiG-21s escorted Su-7s on close support missions in the Shakargar bulge and Chhamb sectors and on the 8th, while escorting 4 Su-7s, the two escorting MiG-21s were at last bounced by two Mirage IIIs coming in from 7 o'clock. A prompt hard climbing turn into them soon had the MiG-21s behind the Mirages but a misunderstood call had the Mirages going into escape manoeuvres. A probable kill was however recorded the next day over Pathankot when 4 Mirage struck Pathankot. Capping

Tigers were behind the Mirages as they exited at low level and two K-13A air-to-air missiles were fired, with at least one hitting. The striken Mirage was reported as disappearing off the screen in Pakistan's territory, south west of Pathankot.

Intense flying continued day after day, and by December 12, 347 missions had been flown by the Tigers (averaging 40 per day) the ground crew making herculean efforts round the clock to maintain the Tigers at 100 per cent serviceability.

Enemy air activity dwindled each passing day even as the IAF continued its relentless strikes and fighter sweeps particularly over the bulge. On December 15 not a single PAF aircraft was reported in the skies over West Punjab, inspite of many high level sweeps over vital areas. By December 17, at ceasefire, No.1 Squadron had flown a total of 518 operational sorties, or nearly 20 per cent of the total number flown by Western Air Command throughout the 14-day war!

The CO Wg Cdr Upkar Singh was awarded the AVSM, Sqn Ldr S Subbaramu the VrC and there were a host of VMs and mention-in despatches. During the momentous year 1971, the Tigers had not only earned laurels in war but had maintained an incredibly high standard of flight safety and serviceability. Not a single aircraft was lost, in war or peace.

No. 1 Squadron continued to be based at Adampur for the next ten years, Upkar Singh as Commanding Officer till September 24, 1973, when he handed over the Tigers to Wg Cdr Brijesh Jayal, a highly qualified test pilot and later destined to become Commodore Commandant of No.1 Squadron and an Air Marshal at the time of the Tigers' Diamond Jubilee.

After Brijesh Jayal's tenure, the reins of No.1 were assumed by Wg Cdr Keith Lewis on February 17, 1976 for over two years, then by Wg Cdr T Sen who was succeeded by Wg Cdr PR Jaindass from January 1981 to May 1983. It was in this tenure that the Tigers celebrated their Golden Jubilee, the Squadron meanwhile having been relocated at Gorakhpur in February 1982, after a record period of stay at Adampur. The Commodore Commandant on April 1, 1983 was Air Marshal TS Brar who had commanded No.1 Squadron in 1953 and the occasion saw venerable Tigers mixing with young ones, a historic and nostalgic occasion.

Shortly thereafter, Wg Cdr TJ Master became CO, till August 24, 1984, when he handed over No. 1 Squadron to Wg Cdr GK Viswanathan, the Tigers soon moving even further east, to Hashimara, in the eastern Dooars, in 1985. The premier Squadron of the Indian Air Force had been flying the weary MiG-21 FL for nearly twenty years (another record) and it was about time for re-equipment. The Chief of Air Staff was now Air Chief Marshal Lakshman Katre, who, as a young Flying Officer, had in 1947 brought the Squadron's ground party from Peshawar by train. His fondness for the Tigers was certainly evident in the selection of No. 1 Squadron to receive the brand new, advanced technology, Mirage 2000 digital delta.

Tigers and the Mirage 2000

For four decades, every succeeding generation of fighter-types with the Indian Air Force seems to have had, as genesis in their selection process, 'inspiration' from across the border! The Mysteres in 1956 were ordered in response to Sabres with the PAF. The MiG-21s in 1963 in response to Starfighters and the Mirage 2000s ordered in 1982 were the IAF's response to induction of F-16 Fighting Falcons by the PAF.

In October 1982, the Government of India formalized

orders for 40 Dassault Mirage 2000s, the advanced multi-role delta-winged fighter with fly-by-wire flight controls, multi-mode radar and beyond-visual-range air-to-air missiles. As with the Mystere IVAs in 1956, specially selected pilots, technical officers and men were sent to France, the first batch arriving on November 1984 and attached to the Armee de I'Air Base at Mont de Marson, in the scenic Bordeaux country. The IAF became the first foreign air arm to receive the new generation Mirage 2000 and the IAF personnel were to convert on the type via simulator time with the French Air Force at Dijon, where No. 1 Squadron's pilots had been posted nearly three decades earlier, in October 1956.

The Government of India had sanctioned the raising of two new fighter Squadrons for operating the Mirage 2000 but the IAF's top brass had correctly considered that the Service's premier Squadrons must be honoured to receive this advanced new fighter type. Thus, Nos. 1 and 7 Squadrons were chosen to re-equip with the Mirage 2000 and their MiG-21s then being operated 'transferred' to the newly created Nos. 52 and 51 Squadrons respectively.

The first seven Mirage 2000s for the Indian Air Force left from Bordeaux-Merignac on their ferry flight to India on June 21, 1985, led by Wg Cdr Ajit Bhavnani, CO designate of the 'Battle Axe' Squadron, arriving at their permanent new airbase at Gwalior on June 28. Amongst the first seven were Sqn Ldrs Padamjit Singh Ahluwalia, NA Moitra, SU Apte and Anil Chopra, all destined to command No.1 Squadron with the Mirage 2000 in the following years.

After six months of Mirage operations in India, the Maharajpur airbase was to witness a 'mass defection' from the Battle Axe ranks to those of the Tigers when, on January

1, 1986, No. 1 Squadron formally came into being at Gwalior, with eleven pilots joining and the 'Tiger One' (Wg Cdr PS Ahluwalia) ensuring that their DSS Hanger was excellently done up to mark the occasion. All the Squadron records, albums, trophies (including the stuffed Tiger) had been flown in from Hashimara for the Squadron's museum. No.1 Squadron commenced normal operational flying from the very next day and a scorching pace was literally set. With the Squadron achieving a commendable 220 hours of flying in the very first month of operation with the new fighter.

The Tigers were to shoulder the prime responsibility for the country's air defence and over the next few years, honed their new mounts into a formidable fighting machine. The excellent radar/missile combination (Thomson-CSF RDM airborne radar and Matra Super R530D beyond-visual-range missile) and advanced electronic warfare systems have made the Mirage 2000H into an awesome weapon system. No. 1 Squadron's Mirages have exercised with almost all contemporary combat aircraft types in India's inventory, including the MiG-29 air superiority fighter and the Navy's Sea Harrier V/STOL lighter.

After exactly 29 months of command, Wg Cdr PS Ahluwalia handed over the Tigers' reins to Wg Cdr SU Apte, who commanded No. 1 Squadron till April 1990, his place being taken by the Tigers for exactly two years before handing over to Wg Cdr Anil Chopra on April 24, 1992, on whose able hands the Squadron has flown into its Diamond Jubilee.

12

LEST WE FORGET

It was during World War I (1914-1918) that the Indian Army for the first time fought a first class European Army. It had the opportunity to prove itself in countless battles in Europe, Asia and Africa. The number of troops sent by the Indian Army to various Fronts up to October, 1918 was 1,302,394. Of these, over 55,000 died in battles and thousands were wounded. It was during this war that Indians were made eligible for the coveted gallantry award of Victoria Cross in recognition of their outstanding performance. India Gate in New Delhi was built as a Memorial for those who fell fighting during 1914-1918, and all their names are inscribed on it.

This was a major turning point in the history of Indian Defence Forces. They had made a point and the British were quick to appreciate the positive fighting qualities of the Indians, not forgetting their loyalty and amenability to discipline with little or hardly any fancy demands in battle conditions. It suited them fine and did a lot good to us, and helped us to be a sturdy, never-say-die fighting force we are today.

□

During World War II, the Indian Defence Forces once again had shown exemplary valour and heroism in as diverse theatres of war as Sahara Desert, Arakans and the trenches of Tobruk. An army which was, till their induction into the World War II, only braced for enemy across the Khyber Pass, had come out as one of the best Standing Armies of the world after World War II.

The British knew it.

The British acknowledged it.

The British were proud of it because it was their trained Army and they had worked hard to make it a professional fighting force. They had reasons to be happy.

The war had cost the world 50 million dead, two-thirds among them civilians. The shock waves that this war sent through our societies have yet not died away.

When the war had started the Indian Army was not geared up to the role it was called upon to perform. The Army had been primarily intended for the defence of the country from any invasion from the North West. As long as the British Fleet was strong in the Indian Ocean, it was felt that, there was no threat to the security of the long coastline. The Northern and Eastern Frontiers were also not threatened by any powerful enemies.

When the war broke out in September 1939, the total strength of the Indian Army was – 15,900 British troops, 18,700 Gurkhas, and 1,25,800 Indian troops. The Indian Army was not mechanised, lacked mobility and possessed the obsolete discarded weapons. It had remained virtually unchanged till World War II because the British saw no threat to justify a more modernized and a better equipped Indian Army.

In the initial stages of war, there was little impact on India, but as the war progressed and the Japanese joined the fray there was an overnight change in the perceptions and threat scenarios. By the time the war ended, the Army strength in India and overseas had risen to 2,644,323 including 2,40,613 men of the British Army.

The Indians fought virtually in every theatre of operations. They claimed innumerable battle honours and won Victoria Crosses, the ultimate accolade for a soldier. But it was closer home that they really came to their own. The Battle of lmphal was perhaps their Finest Hour. They were the backbone of General Orde Wingate's Chindits who chased the Japanese out of Burma, pushed them southwards and hastened the final surrender.

The infrastructure apart, the Indian *Faujis* performed with elan in many theatres of war, forcing even the ever caustic Sir Winston Churchill to acknowledge:

The glorious heroism and martial qualities of the Indian troops—the unsurpassed bravery of Indian soldiers, both Hindus and Moslems, will shine for ever in the annals of war.

General Slim had stated:

My Indian Divisions after 1943 were among the best in the world. They would go anywhere, do anything, and go on doing it—and do it on very little.

In Burma, besides the Indian Divisions there were Africans, British, Chinese and Burmese Divisions under Field Marshal William Slim. According to General Slim the Indian Divisions were the best of the lot. Out of the 27 Victoria Crosses awarded for various actions in Burma, 20 were conferred on Indians.

Quite a compliment considering the fact that the British always kept some distance from the natives as an Imperial Power and certainly had rather high standards of professionalism. Speaks volumes for the performance of our ancestors. Happily, this is something we haven't forgotten and have always tried to emulate their acts of achieving results no matter what the odds.

□

Nos. 4 and 5 Indian Divisions, No. 1 Squadron, IAF, HMIS Bengal are some of the many formations that distinguished themselves. Indian soldiers and officers covered themselves with glory and the Roll Call of Honour includes well-known names like General Bhagat's Victoria Cross, General Rajindra Singhji's DSO, Air Chief Marshal (now Marshal) Arjan Singh's DFC and Admiral Krishnan's DSC among a string of gallantry awards won by us.

The price was heavy. The most severe was in Malaya where nearly 70,000 officers and men were taken as prisoners after the surrender of Singapore and had to undergo immense privations and inhuman cruelty. Our total casualties add up to 1,75,000 officers and men. Nearly 20,000 were killed in action.

The Indian Air Force and Navy were not behind in their effort. Before the war, IAF was a tiny service with about 200 officers and men manning three Flights of No. 1 Squadron. By 1945 the Service had 9 Squadrons and a strength of 1638 officers and 26,900 men. They flew over 16,000 sorties in Burma alone involving more than 24,000 hours of flying. The contribution of No. 1 Squadron was by far the most outstanding—out of 22 Distinguished Flying Crosses (DFCs) awarded to IAF, No. 1 had bagged 9 DFCs.

The Royal Indian Navy in September 1939 had 114 commissioned officers and 1475 Ratings. Naval Headquarters was manned by 13 officers. By the time war ended, the strength of Navy had risen to 27,651.

Despite the sterling performance by the Indian Armed Forces during World War II, and the glowing tributes while the war lasted, the recorded history, unjustifiably, gives the Indians a nearly Also-Ran status. Nevertheless, this is understandable because the western historians of the era have recorded the events from the Imperial perspective. The Colonial historians could hardly be expected to elevate the native effort and contribution beyond a point without compromising the British performance.

What is painful and regrettable is our own official approach to the post independence war history of India. It has tended to consider the military inheritance from the British as colonial lackeys. Since independence Indian Army has lost over 17,000 soldiers while nearly 30,000 were wounded. This is spread over four major wars and Special Operations like Blue Star (Punjab), Operation Pawan (Sri Lanka) and Meghdoot (Siachen), and counter insurgency operations in the North East, Kashmir, UN Missions and Aid to Civil Power.

BRAVERY

Real bravery inspired by devotion to duty does not know panic.

Ardant du Picq

President Dr. Zakir Hussain and Air Chief Marshal Arjan Singh at the Standard Presentation Ceremony to No. 1 Squadron, IAF

13

DIVISION OF ARMED FORCES

The year of 1940 stands as a Turning Point in the history of India. It was in this year that Muslim League formally adopted the idea of a separate homeland for the Muslims of India as its objective. The movement had gained such a momentum that by the end of 1946 the creation of Pakistan had become inevitable.

This had raised the question of the future of Armed Forces of British India:

- Whether the subcontinent would continue to be treated as one unit as far as defence was concerned, and the new States of India and Pakistan have a Joint Control of the Armed Forces, OR
- Would the Armed Forces be also divided along with the division of the subcontinent.

The British Officers generally regarded the idea of division of the existing structure and organisation of the Armed Forces as painful. They delayed it until the political conditions compelled them to change their mind. Thus, not only the preparation of the formula of the division of the Armed Forces, but also the actual division had to be carried out in a period of 72 days as a last resort when all efforts to keep them united had failed.

□

When the Muslim League had put forward the idea of the division of the Armed Forces, the British Government had not welcomed it. The British High Command was of the opinion that the division of the Armed Forces would be suicidal for an institution which they and their predecessors had established with the hard labour of about two centuries. Undeniably, they had a very soft corner for the Indian Armed Forces with which they had such a long and a fruitful association.

The British had argued that the Armed Forces of India and Pakistan would not be able to attain the degree of efficiency which marked the organisation of the British Indian Armed Forces. Field Marshal Sir Claude Auchinleck, Commander-in-Chief, was particularly opposed to such a move to divide the force. He believed that the Indian Armed Forces must be maintained as an undivided and over-all defence force.

The British had some very good reasons for their view. They knew that while the Indians had proved to be excellent fighters, they lacked the higher command expertise which was rather limited, and which was bound to be further adversely affected if there was a further division of their meagre number of senior officers.

The British officers were of the view that the division of the Armed Forces would put both India and Pakistan on road of administrative chaos and leave the subcontinent defenceless. The broken and confused units might start killing the followers of opposite religions. This view was also supported by the British Press. *Glasgow Herald* had commented:

If any attempt is made to divide the Indian Army, it is bound to disintegrate in a welter of blood. This will be the beginning of the real civil war—law, order, communication, industry, trade and even farming will cease and India will be back in the days of break-up of Mughal Empire from which she was rescued by the British.

The British owned English language paper of India, *The Statesman*, had editorially commented that such a step would be disastrous:

Asia for several decades had only three First Class Armies—The Russian, The Indian and The Japanese. The first and the second of the three emerged victorious from the recent war, and third was beaten. Should second now for communal reasons fall to pieces, lowering India's two parts Hindustan and Pakistan to the military level of perhaps Siam and Iraq. The global strategic balance would be disrupted and repercussions in power politics will be felt in every continent.

All efforts to keep the Armed Forces united proved futile. A last minute effort to preserve the unity of Armed Forces was made by a few senior officers. Brigadier KM Cariappa (later Field Marshal) contacted the Muslim officers to secure their support for the proposal to keep the Armed Forces united, but the response was not encouraging.

□

The division of troops was completed without much difficulty. By August 15, 1947, the future of the Units had been decided. The Units under the Punjab Boundary Force and the troops overseas had escaped the division on communal cum territorial basis.

□

Happily, the fears expressed by different quarters that the division of the Armed Forces between India and Pakistan would result in an administrative chaos, proved to be unfounded. They coped with the immediate and the subsequent tasks admirably despite their lack of experience.

Immediate Task

Immediately after Independence while the Armed Forces of India and Pakistan were undergoing the process of reconstitution and nationalization, communal situation deteriorated and the Indo-Pak subcontinent witnessed horrors and tragedies which were enacted to gain political aims by violence and murder. The Armed Forces had to be called out in various places to maintain law and order and save the lives of the innocent victims of riots and restore the authority of the civil administration.

The situation worsened especially in Punjab after the announcement of the Partition Plan. The wave of killing, looting, arson, rape and torture enveloped the subcontinent. A special Military Command under General TW Rese—The Punjab Boundary Force—was created by the government on August 1, 1947, to safeguard peace in the Districts of Sialkot, Gujranwala, Sheikhpura, Lyallapur, Montgomery, Lahore, Gurdaspur, Hoshiarpur, Amritsar, Jullunder, Ferozepur and Ludhiana. It consisted of 50,000 troops of 4th Indian Division (less 7th Brigade), 14th Parachute, the 53rd Lorried and 14th Infantry Brigades.

The Punjab Boundary Force had a mixed composition with the Muslims and non-Muslims ratio of 35:65. But the communal situation had deteriorated to such an extent that the task grew out of proportion to the responsibility originally placed on its shoulders. The Joint Defence Council had to abolish the Boundary Force from the night of August 31/ September 1, 1947. The riot affected areas were handed over to the Dominion concerned, each having full control of the area within its territory.

The two Governments had handed over the evacuation of refugees and their protection to their Armed Forces. The troops provided protection to refugee convoys of their co-religionists moving across the frontier on foot, carts, buses and trains. They were also given the task to establish, manage and protect the camps in co-operation with the civil authorities, and provide shelter, food, clothing and medical facilities to them. They also maintained law and order in disturbed areas by clearing them of the raiders. In Autumn 1947, floods which swept across Punjab, further worsened the conditions under which refugees were living. The Army Engineers and Sappers came forward to help. The Navy and the Air Force helped in moving the troops and refugees by sea and air.

The task before the Armed Forces was even more difficult than it appeared. The mutual suspicion and lack of co-operation between the new governments of India and Pakistan, the disruption of the means of communications which came in the way of movement of troops from one trouble spot to another, not forgetting the enormous influx of refugees, made the matters worse. On many occasions there were pitched battles between the troops and the raiders and on certain occasions the army arrived when the raiders had disappeared after killing almost the whole population of the village. The general morale of the troops was not high because many of them were worried about the welfare of their own kith and kin.

No exact figures are available about those killed in riots. Various unofficial estimates differ from each other. But one thing is quite clear. It was an unprecedented massacre and exodus. No doubt the Armed Forces could not totally control the situation but they did their best under the circumstances and constraints. Often the nationalist feelings were overwhelming and this led to an unfair handling in some crucial areas. But if the Armed Forces had remained silent spectators to the holocaust, the results would have been a lot more painful and ghoulish.

PAKISTAN

It is inevitable for India and Pakistan to have close relations; very close relations. We can be either hostile or very friendly with each other. Ultimately we can only be really very friendly, whatever period of hostility may intervene, because our interests are closely interlinked.

Jawaharlal Nehru

14

THE DAYS AFTER INDEPENDENCE

The partition of the country had resulted in the uprooting of millions of people from their homes apart from looting, carnage, rape and murder on an unprecedented scale in history. This is something that the leaders on both the sides of the divide had not visualised—not the scale and the suddenness with which the volcano erupted.

On the day after Independence, the Boundary Commission published its report on the borders of the partitioned provinces of Punjab and Bengal. It shocked the whole nation. Muslims were livid with rage, and the Sikhs, who had voted for partition, flew to arms to oppose it; for the rich lands of western Punjab with its vital power supply, and the great city of Lahore had been given to Pakistan.

The communal fighting had begun even before the Independence day, but the report touched off the most horrible massacres of all. The Punjab Boundary Force of 50,000 men, organised by Lord Mountbatten under the command of British General TW Reese, was helpless to combat it. Its efforts to restore order brought the hatred of both sides upon it, and it was disbanded in late August, 1947.

So shocking were the reports of the carnage in Punjab

that Pandit Jawaharlal Nehru had dropped everything else to fly there on August 17, two days after Independence. He was joined in Punjab by the Prime Minister of Pakistan, Mr Liaquat Ali Khan. Although they worked together to try and check the killings, they could not.

The slaughter and fear of worse to come started the greatest mass migration of the people in the history of the world. Millions of panic-stricken Muslims fled across the Punjab plains towards Pakistan encountering hordes of Hindus and Sikhs heading for India. These people had abandoned their homes and lands, on which some of them had lived for countless generations, and taking their portable possessions and their cattle, if they had any, started off in two wheeled bullock-carts or on foot, carrying their children, their sick and their old in their arms or on their backs, joining others in columns sixty miles long over which choking dust of dry roads rose like pillars of clouds.

Nor were they allowed to go in peace. In East Punjab bands of armed Hindus and Sikhs rose out of the fields to attack Muslim refugees, killing under their blood stained swords till they became too heavy for their weary arms to lift. While in West Punjab, the hate ridden Muslims slaughtered the columns of Hindus and Sikhs. Even the special trains which had been arranged to run between the two countries were hardly spared.

There are no reliable statistics on the great panic migrations or the number of people killed, but the most conservative estimate is that over 6000,000 Muslims, and 4,500,000 Hindus and Sikhs moved from one country to the other, and of these 200,000 to 700,000 were killed. One hundred thousand girls were stolen and sold to the highest bidder.

15

INDIAN DEFENCE FORCES

Three Unique Features

The Defence Forces occupy a distinctive position in the new nations. They maintain a national outlook. They are more oriented to western practices and technology. Above all, they control the Instrument of Violence. The Defence Forces are more organised than most civilian institutions and are characterized by their centralization, hierarchy, discipline, inter-communication and *esprit de corps.*

There are three unique features that make Defence Forces distinctive and dynamic:

FIRST, most of the organisations except the military operate within the context of their own society. The military constantly looks outside the country—towards developed military powers. This makes them aware of international standards and the latest developments in the military strategy. This is especially so in the initial stages.

The recruits coming mostly from rural areas, are educated, trained and disciplined in particular skills. The officers are trained in military institutions established/

patterned on western concepts. They study and learn technology and principles of warfare of industrially developed nations. It is one of the key mechanisms which a nation possesses for receiving and sometimes amplifying signals from its external environment—these signals include Ideas, Values, Skills, Techniques and Strategies. This in turn makes the Defence Forces quite conscious of the relative backwardness of their society.

SECOND, the political leadership of most new nations recognize the need to maintain strong and efficient Armed Forces to defend and protect the territorial integrity of the state from the actual or potential internal or external threats. The liberal allocation of funds enables the Armed Forces to acquire modern equipment and technological skills. Thus, they represent a modernized organisation in a relatively less developed society.

Sadly, the importance of the Armed Forces has not been wholly understood by our political leadership. It would appear that the guiding factor has been the fear of a military coup. While the Indian leadership did well to keep the Armed Forces apolitical, but they went to the other extreme by keeping them ill-equipped, ill-treated, embarrassed and humiliated. This certainly had an adverse effect on our preparedness, and even today we seem to chase the acquisitions by Pakistan instead or arming ourselves befitting our size and status in South Asia. However, 1962 Debacle notwithstanding, the Indian Defence Forces have kept up their traditions of valour and risen up to the occasion despite the handicaps, and carried the day.

THIRD, military is not merely a profession; it is a way of life. Our training is so thorough that it replaces parochial and particularistic orientation of its members and inculcates identification with the national symbol and military's professional corporate identity. This contributes to discipline and cohesion in the military which is reinforced by keeping the military at a little distance from the rest of the society.

Thus, in a fragmented and indisciplined society, the Armed Forces maintain an integrated organisation, a national outlook and knowledge of comparatively modern technology. As they stay at a distance from the civil society, their public image is high. They are considered honest, patriotic, firm and a symbol of national sovereignty.

Under the British

The military was organised on the modern lines by the British. It was in 1895 that the three armies of the Presidencies of Bombay, Calcutta and Madras were amalgamated and put under the C-in-C of India. The Indian Navy and the Indian Air Force were reorganised as independent forces in 1928 and 1933 respectively. These were smaller services in comparison to the Army and were inadequate for the defence of India except in collaboration with the Royal Navy and the Royal Air Force. Much of their expansion took place during World War II, which was indeed a turning point. The British emphasized the principle of civilian supremacy over the military. The ultimate control of the Indian Army was with the British government in London. In India, the military and the government of British India were more of equal partners. Both were responsible to the British government for efficient functioning and performance in their respective spheres.

Evolution

We have inherited a highly distinguished peace and war record from the legends of our recent past. They brought brilliant victories for the British in Africa, Europe and Far East during World War II. Eventhough we were not so well equipped as the western armies, our courage and fidelity more than made up for this while confronting the Japanese and the German armies. The victories at El-Alamein, Italy and Burma are a testimony to the dauntless courage of our ancestors and the high standards they have set for us to emulate.

In Burma, besides the Indian Divisions there were Africans, British, Chinese and Burmese Divisions under Field Marshal William Slim. According to him, the Indian Divisions were the best of the lot. Of the 27 Victoria Crosses awarded for various 'Actions' in Burma, 20 were conferred on Indians. That is the kind of heritage we have inherited and have to live up to.

Except for the Air Force, a creation of last seventy years or so, our Army has evolved over a number of centuries. Both Army and Navy served the East India Company and indeed 'John Company' took over some of the forces of the decayed Mughal Empire. There are Army units which can trace their histories back to a couple of centuries. For example, the defeat of the very fine armies of Ranjit Singh led to their incorporation in John Company's forces of Sikh soldiers. These, subsequently, found their way into the British Indian Army, and later after Partition, into our own.

These units helped British fight their wars all over the world. They helped in subjugation of what was left of Mughal Raj. A large majority of these units contained the ancestors of those soldiers who are now serving the Indian Army. They served the Mughals, the Sikhs, the French and the British to the best of their ability for as long as they were paid regularly. In fact, it has been stated that the British won their Indian

Empire by making sure that their soldiers were regularly paid.

An Appraisal

An overview of the Indian Defence Forces today would suggest a general lowering of standards, and make no mistake about it. But, happily, the rate of slide has been gradual primarily because of our traditions of valour and integrity which are hammered in and ingrained in the men right from the day they join the training establishments and they are rather difficult to get over more so when our men are challenged. That is good news.

However, there is an urgent need to carry out an objective assessment of general decline of standards and various other factors. Just the rhetoric, 'We are the best in the world', could boomerang unless we learn our lessons fast and take remedial measures, something that we are not quite good at and prefer to rather put the problems away under the carpet.

It is very tempting and easy to blame the politicians and the bureaucrats for all our ills, as also the fall in the moral standards of the society, but there are many things that could be set right by the leadership within the Defence Forces itself—for example, trying to lead by personal example; by trying to be a teacher rather than a critic. This good old style of leading men in peace and war has been wiped out by the five star culture of many of our leaders who assume it to be their right. Of course, rank and position do confer certain perks on the commanders but they must keep their feet on the ground and not get lost in cloud-nine.

There are two distinct segments of the Army. One is the Regimental Army up to the Unit level which forms its backbone. Patriotism, Fidelity, Comradeship and Service-Before-Self are still the norms in the 'Real Army', which remain well-disciplined, efficient and effective.

The other is the small group which constitutes the seniors and the top leadership. Unhappily, this is the one which has shown lack of leadership qualities and professional integrity required to lead your men in peace and war. It takes major decisions which effect the rank and file and therefore, any ill-advised or not well considered actions tend to erode the morale of the defence forces.

The junior lot has been a fast learner. They have realized that it is far easier to get promotions by selling their loyalty to up and coming senior officers. That's bad news. The credibility gap between the senior ranks and the Regimental/ Unit segments has increased. There has been a gradual decline in discipline among the junior ranks as they find their seniors and superiors not willing to protect their interests and not being able to walk their impassioned-talks written by their speech writers much like the politicians.

DISCIPLINE

When his troops are disorderly, the General has no prestige.

Chen Hao

Good order is the foundation of all things.

Edmud Burke

The discipline and training suffer from the decline in the efficiency of officers.

De Gaulle

16

THE HIMALAYAN BLUNDER: THE UNFOUGHT WAR OF 1962

An Overview

Tension had been mounting on the Northern Borders from 1958 onwards. In late 1962, troops were hurriedly sent forward to the international border. Their main source of supply was air maintenance by the Air Force. The Army had asked for heavy air drops of badly needed stores at Tsangdhar (in NEFA). The DZ (Dropping Zone) was on a steep slope at a height of 14,500 ft Southeast of the tri-junction of China, Bhutan and India, across the Namka Chu gorge on the Thagla ridge. Though the Dakota was the most suitable aircraft for these drops, the Packet had to be pressed into service for the tricky task in view of the magnitude of supply drops required. Regular air drops by Packets from Guwahati had started on October 5, 1961. The same story was being repeated in other sectors, till October 20 when the transport aircraft reported that a regular battle was raging on the Thagla ridge area and that Tsangdhar DZ was being continuously shelled. This was the first intimation of the Chinese attack. A helicopter flown into Tsangdhar by Sqn Ldr VK Sehgal with Major Ram Singh and Corporal K Kumar was lost in this operation along with the crew. They were the first martyrs of the 1962 war.

From then onwards the Air Force had a formidable task. It had to transport troops and stores, evacuate casualties and maintain air supply in the hazardous mountainous regions of both Ladakh and NEFA and it went headlong with everything it had by way of transport and helicopters. But the time was too short, the terrain most forbidding and resources inadequate for the troops to withstand the massive thrust of the Chinese which was pre-planned and extremely well-organised.

The Chinese aggression was a traumatic experience which forced the country to have a still closer look at its defence preparedness. It also had an ominous repercussion in that it encouraged another aggression against India a little later.

Use of Air Power

The use of Air Power immediately after the Chinese had launched their offensive in Ladakh and NEFA, would have made a lot of difference, and would have certainly changed the course of the battle. But, the idea was most casually, indeed, cavalierly, dismissed.

The question of active participation of the Indian Air Force, both fighter and transport support, was first raised when Chinese had surrounded in the summer of 1962, Indian Posts in the Galwan and Chip Chap Valleys of Ladakh, and were threatening to over-run them. The Government had then ordered that these isolated and vulnerable Posts be reinforced by 'Air', using helicopters and aircrafts as well. Everyone was convinced of the idea's soundness, but no one dared to raise the matter in the presence of Prime Minister, Pandit

Jawaharlal Nehru or the Defence Minister, Mr VK Krishna Menon.

At the same time a whispering campaign was started (By whom?) that the use of Air Force in support of ground troops would invite Chinese bombing of Indian cities, while our bombers will not be able to reach any worthwhile targets in Tibet, leave alone mainland China. It was on this specious ground that the proposal to use air power in support of ground troops was not even entertained when the war began.

The unanswered question is, the only person who could have given his professional advice to the Government and told that the Chinese were in no position to effectively operate any bombers from the airfields in Tibet at that time because of the high altitude at which these airfields were located. The Chinese aircraft didn't have the range to reach Delhi. In any case, the flight would have exposed the Chinese aircraft to a hostile environment during their long flight over our territory. This point could have been effectively made by the Air Chief. DID HE?

In one of his 'Down The Memory Lane' articles, says Air Chief Marshal (now Marshal) Arjan Singh (Retd):

"*I am often asked why we did not take offensive in 1962 Operations when our Army was attacked by the Chinese. The Air Force took part in a big way in supply dropping (and casualty evacuation) operations. However, it was decided by the government that no offensive air action would be undertaken. Had we done so with our fighter and bomber units in the crucial fighting even in two or three places, I think the outcome would have been somewhat different. In my opinion it was a mistake (not to use IAF in offensive role). We had adequate amount of Air Force and arrangements in the Assam Valley, and we had the capability to use the Air Force effectively from air bases which were almost at sea level, a big advantage against Chinese operating at bases at 14000 feet or so."*

The question still remains unanswered. Did the government go against the professional advice given by the Air Chief, or, NO professional advice was asked for, therefore not given?.

Eventually, after the ignominious withdrawal from Sela Pass around third week of November, 1962, the Indian Prime Minister, Pandit Jawaharlal Nehru, had written a letter to the American President, John F Kennedy, asking for participation of the United States Air Force in defence of India. The specific request was for twelve Squadrons of F-104s, and two Squadrons of B-57 bombers.

Was the request made on the professional advice of the IAF?

Had the IAF expressed its inability to protect its skies against the possible Chinese air attack? Or, was it a political decision?

A Military Debacle and a Political Disaster

While the nation is still looking forward to the official version of our (NONE?) performance in 1962, we had a number of books written by Army officers and bureaucrats giving their own versions, justifications, not forgetting self-glorification. Nevertheless, the nation still continues to grope for the answers to the numerous unanswered questions.

Was it really a case of cowardice?

Or, was it rank bad leadership?

Can we rule out treason or still worse, string pulling to put India in the corner where the concerned countries felt, it belonged and bring it down from the high pedestal it had been trying to occupy with its policy of non-alignment?

What really went wrong?

Our performance in the eastern sector leaves gaping holes in the justifications and the reasons put forth so far, for the debacle. The nation does deserve to know the facts. It is too late to catch the wrong guys because, most of them perhaps have already faded away, but it can certainly help us to draw the right lessons and not make the same mistakes again. The answers provided so far are too contrived, and don't pass even a simple test of truth.

We have officially learnt the fine art of making full use of the short human memory, our total lack of interest in defence matters, and history as such. Just a look at the published historical records, if any since 1947, will show what I mean. The only records we seem to have are the personal records, opinions and scenarios based on imaginary or at the best a limited access to facts.

If you remember those harrowing days of 1962 Sino-Indian Conflict, there are a few questions that had kept cropping up and, as usual, no answers were forthcoming. The result was an over-active Rumour Mill which was working overtime, and yet we were nowhere near the truth. Let us look back in sorrow to see if we can figure out the truth.

What Went Wrong at Sela?

Everything. We just ran, and kept running.

One could accept and even condone the initial reverses because of our poor appreciation of the Chinese intentions. But having dug-in, and moved-in our well-determined, well-clothed and well-armed army on the Sela heights, whereby all accounts we held all the aces, it is rather hard to accept our dismal performance.

We were so sure of our strength and ability to avenge our thrashing by the Chinese in other areas, that we had felt confident enough to take the VIPs and the Media to Sela Pass, to let them have a look themselves. And there was, rather were, many good reasons for it. We were certainly on a firm ground and the troops were itching to have a go at it, and flex their muscles, for a change, from a position of strength.

Then, what went wrong at Sela? The question remains unanswered even today. What we have are only half-truths and half-answers, when, perhaps, there are many deeper undercurrents. Why have we been reluctant to get at the solid facts?

Why did we give up without a fight, in fact, even before a single shot was fired by the Chinese, or even by us? We were well-stocked to fight for fifteen days and maintained by 'Air'. We had the added advantage of having beaten back the Chinese on November 17, 1962. We had the superiority over the Chinese in numbers, weaponry, supply system and the quality of troops—all were from reputed Regiments with a reputation to fight till the last man. We were on the home ground, well dug-in, determined and itching to take on the enemy.

THEN. Why did we run? Circumstances leading to the abandoning of well organised and defended Sela position, is still a mystery (or, is it really?), and we as a nation seem to have done little to get at the truth. We seem to have mastered the art of dodging the inconvenient questions even if they concern the national security.

Let us hear the Sela Story from Lt Col JR Saigal, who was a part of the force at Sela. I share with you the excerpt from his book *The Unfought War Of 1962*. So, tighten your seat-belt because what you are going to read is the first person true account which has not been disputed till date, and might make you feel angry, very very angry, for the higher formations having been so callous, timid, or was it an invisible hand which made us give up the fight for whatever reason(s).

"The real sad story starts on November 18, 1962. I rang up Major Wadke, the BM (Brigade Major) and inquired from him about the latest situation. I had been aware about the confusion prevailing in the Divisional Headquarters when I had returned to my Brigade the previous evening.

Brigadier AS Cheema, Commander, 65 Infantry Brigade, had gone to the Divisional Headquarters in the morning and had not yet returned to the Brigade Headquarters. I wanted to know more about the roadblock established by the Chinese near Munna Camp. Infantry Companies had been sent along with tanks to clear the roadblock.

Wadke didn't know anything about the situation.

Sometimes later I saw him talking to Brig AS Cheema outside the Commander's bunker. I didn't know what transpired, and had heard many versions of the conversation later. But I could hear a little later Brig Cheema shouting in a rather incoherent manner, '*MANDALA, MANDALA, BHAGO, BHAGO*', and he appeared terribly excited, and a moment later drove away hurriedly in a jeep!!

There was sudden excitement all around. I could not meet the Commander that morning as he had left in such a hurry. There was no conference as would have been normal before he left (FLED?). I went back to my tent, put on the equipment and pistol, and came out. I saw Maj Wadke talking to some men who had gathered there.

A moment later, there was sudden confusion.

Just a while ago the BM was talking to the Camp personnel, and now everyone had started running helter-skelter across the stream to the neighbouring Field Ambulance Area.

I had shouted to stop them from running, as running on such occasions would create confusion and panic. A few personnel stopped. Others continued to run-on. All types of rumours were afloat among them.

Naik Kunwar Bahadur, who heard me shouting came to me and said that some of our men had fired. I had heard only one or two rounds fired during the confusion. Suddenly someone seemed to have kindled a smoke bomb near the stream, and this had caused further confusion and panic.

I took up a position and looked all around. Naik Kunwar Bahadur took position near me. There could be no Chinese anywhere near as the Marathas were on one side and our own troops (Medical troops) on the other side.

By this time the flight was in full swing and soon I found no one on the open patch of ground where there were over fifty men just a few minutes back! Someone had started shouting '*BHAGO*', possibly after hearing the Brigade Commander shouting the same word, and hastily driving away.

A full-fledged operational Brigade Headquarters, the nerve centre of nearly three thousand troops under its command, had disintegrated in a few minutes (without a shot being fired). We had left behind everything intact—wireless sets, telephones, important operational stores etc. Not only that, the Brigade Commander and the Brigade Major had fled, leaving behind the remaining troops to fend for themselves.

NOT A SINGLE CHINESE WAS ANYWHERE WITHIN SIGHT NOR A SINGLE CHINESE WEAPON HAD BEEN FIRED AT US.

Then, why did this happen?

Was it an act of sabotage?

Cowardice?

Fear?

As we proceed with the story, it is interesting to note that, the Brigade Commander was only following the Divisional Commander like a good soldier. According to the story, the moment the Brigade Commander had seen the Divisional Commander (Major General AS Pathania, MVC, MC) fleeing, he had made up his mind what is good for him. In fact, it was on the sane and good advice of his driver that the Brigadier had come back to the Brigade Headquarters, and stayed there long enough to say, '*MANDALA, MANDALA, BHAGO, BHAGO*', and after that promptly sped away (as fast as he could).

Let us see what happened at the Divisional Headquarters. Says Lt Col JR Saigal:

"In the Divisional Headquarters, the General Officer Commanding (GOC) abandoned his force early in the morning on November 18, 1962, in his jeep driven by his GSO-2 (Operations). The GOC neither held any conference nor had passed any orders. His GSO-1 had followed him immediately, again without issuing any instructions or even informing his own staff. Not a single shot had been fired by the Chinese, nor was there any sign of Chinese nearby.

YET. The doubly decorated General Officer Commanding deserted his fighting outfit—well organised and superior in force and willing to fight—in a manner, the parallel of which is difficult to find in the annals of military history.

THE COMMAND AND CENTRAL STRUCTURE OF A FORCE OF OVER 15,000 TROOPS WAS PARALYSED IN A MATTER OF MINUTES AND THUS THE WAR WAS LOST UNFOUGHT AT ABOUT 0600 HRS ON NOVEMBER 18,1962.

The Division that had covered itself with glory during the Second World War, and had built up traditions in fighting efficiency, was brought to nought by its own General Officer Commanding and the operational staff."

This is the sad story of SELA.

This is the story told by someone who was a part of the outfit and had the guts to write the book which has not been contradicted till date. The crowning shame was when the guys who should have been punished and court-martialled, were decorated with gallantry awards on the basis of their stories based on the theory of 'Chinese Waves', and how they had bravely repulsed them, when the fact was that, they had not seen a single Chinese soldier, leave aside the waves of them, and fled for whatever reason(s).

The least that the nation deserved after this shameful performance was an honest close-hard look into the battle to make sure that we were not victims of a sabotage from within, as has been hinted by some writers.

□

Air Support: 1962

The Chinese attack on the morning of October 20, 1962, is estimated to have been made by a force of 20,000 men supported by artillery and mortars. We had only two Battalions in the area, 1/9 Gurkhas and 9 Punjabis. 4 Grenadiers were further down near Hathunga Pass. Our troops had no artillery support. We were in a no win situation, and the fall of Thagla ridge was only a matter of time. Brigadier Dalvi, Commander of 7 Brigade did put up a spirited fight but was totally outnumbered and outgunned.

□

The entire North and North-Eastern border is fortified with high Himalayan mountain ranges. These mountain ranges are bisected by small passes at high altitudes. The entire area is covered with thick forests from the plains of Assam to a height of about 8000 ft. Thereafter the ranges are barren till the sowline starts between 14000 and 16000 ft. The Army was deployed in this area.

No. 4 Division was given the task of defending the entire McMahon Line from Bhutan Tri-junction to Burma border, which gave it a Frontage of about 360 miles in the hostile and inhospitable terrain. There were no roads and no laterals. The only access to each area was from Brahamaputra Valley, there were no shelters for the troops and hardly any animal transport. Even the local labour was limited.

During the Sino-Indian Conflict (October 20, 1962 to November 21, 1962) the Indian Air Force gave only transport and logistic support to our troops in these operations, both in the eastern and the western sectors. The combat element was prevented from taking any active part by government for political reasons and wide international repercussions.

The only means of sustaining any force was by air maintenance. At the best of times supplying troops in the forward areas is considered only a temporary affair until the road transport is in a position to take over, unfortunately, however much wasteful and difficult air drops was the only means of maintaining our posts in the area. There were no airfields in the hills where the supplies could be airlanded. The troops used to mark out some dropping zones, but most of them were extremely small and located on mountain slopes. Quite a large percentage of air dropped supplies used to roll into the deep ravines because of the sloping nature of the DZs. On the morning of October 20, 1962, our transport aircraft had taken off for normal supply dropping at Thagla ridge area. They were, however, completely surprised to see the battle raging there. They had quickly realized the seriousness of the situation and turned back.

This was the first intimation of the Chinese attack we got, when they were already there. It was really sudden and unexpected.

A little later in the early morning, a helicopter of the Indian Air Force piloted by Sqn Ldr Sehgal and carrying Maj Ram Singh, Second in Command of the Divisional Signals Regiment had flown into the battle area at Thagla unsuspectingly, and were shot down by the Chinese, killing both the pilot and the passenger.

During the Conflict, 110 Helicopter Unit, IAF based in Assam area gave continuous transport support to the army. It airlifted stores, food supplies, ammunition, medicines and personnel from Darang at the foothills to Zimithang, situated below Lumpu at a height of 2200 meters in support of the Army base which had been established at Lumpu. Initially the aircraft were based at Tezpur but later on one detachment was based at Tawang.

This small helicopter unit which had been recently raised, carried a load of 1500 lbs per sortie, and airlifted about 20,000 lbs of supplies everyday, a remarkable achievement considering the limited number of aircraft available with the unit. The airlift of supplies to Zimithang was carried out till October 21, 1962, after which it was discontinued because of the Chinese threat. Thereafter the airlift was made to Tawany. During the period October 5, 1962 to October 23, 1962 the unit flew a total of 300 hours and airlifted nearly 40,000 lbs of load and 500 personnel in addition to the evacuation of sick and the wounded.

On October 26, 1962, a detachment of this unit was moved to Tezu in Walong Sector to give logistic support to No. III Brigade. The rest of the unit operated from Tezpur to Darang Dzong airlifting ammunition and mines on October 28. The helicopters of this unit were detailed to evacuate retreating troops from Rougtong in Bhutan. During the month of October, the unit flew 420 hours and airlifted 76000 lbs of supplies and nearly 1000 troops. On November 15, 1962, the unit moved to Tezu where during the course of Army Support Operations, one of its helicopters was shot down by enemy ground fire near Walong. From November 22, 1962 onwards, the unit started operating from Amatulla. During this month also the unit carried out intensive flying airlifing nearly 75000 lbs of load and 1300 personnel after the hostilities had ceased. The unit was employed on evacuation of sick and wounded. These operations had carried on till the end of April, 1963.

□

No. 105 Helicopter Unit had carried out a total of 716 operational sorties on various missions of casualty evacuation, reconnaissance, supply dropping, airlifting, arms, ammunition and stores for the troops in forward areas.

During the month of October, the unit carried out sorties to Towang, Zimithang, Shakti, Tsangdhar and Bumla areas. A detachment of the unit operated from Zimithang and carried out casualty evacuation, supply drops and other allied commitments for No. 4 Division which was deployed in the area. In this sector the unit suffered many losses. Sqn Ldr AS William was sent on October 21, 1962, to look for Sqn Ldr Sehgal when he had failed to return to the base. Sqn Ldr William was also shot at by Chinese, and he decided wisely to turn back from Tsangdhar without landing having observed Chinese troops on the ground. His aircraft had been damaged and he had loss of power but he had managed to land on the other side of the hill and ran back to Zimithang. But for his alertness and presence of mind, the unit would have lost another aircraft and an experienced pilot. Afterwards, William who was himself wounded was airlifted by another helicopter of the unit. In the meantime, one officer and eight technicians had been sent to salvage Williams aircraft which was damaged. When they returned to Zimithang, the enemy had already occupied it, and to escape capture, the men had to retreat leaving their belongings back. They had wandered through the ragged mountains for three days without food or shelter eventually linking up with some Army units retreating from the area.

It was a fast moving battle and we seem to have lost all control. The detachment had experienced extreme hardship and suffered mental and physical strain during this period. The unit had lost another precious aircraft at Zimithang when it was hastily abandoned by the army.

□

By first week of November, the first phase of operations in this area was over. The army had withdrawn to Jang Sela in the west and regrouped at Walong in the east. 105 HU was now stationed at Tezpur and had received some new aircraft to make good the losses. The unit kept giving logistic support to our land forces in the area.

On November 15, the Chinese had reached within the striking distance of Walong and the township had to be abandoned by our forces on November 16, 1962. The Helicopter Unit had kept up with their logistic support and other commitments of the army literally from dawn to dusk basis under difficult flying conditions and a hostile environment. They used to carry as many as ten passengers defying all the performance graphs of their fragile aircraft. The courage and the technical skill shown by the pilots was indeed remarkable.

During this period another helicopter was shot down by ground fire but the crew was rescued by another helicopter. This aircraft was on a casualty evacuation mission and had many sick and wounded who were also picked up and rescued.

On November 19, 1962, the unit was given the task of searching for our returning army, supplying them with rations and evacuating the casualties. On November 21, 1962, after a month of virtual string of successes, the Chinese had declared a ceasefire.

The helicopter unit had carried on with its task of trying to search and rescue stragglers in the hills and drop food supplies to the weary troops trying to find their way through hazardous mountain terrain. The pilots had to fly deep into the valleys which were sometimes extremely narrow, to search for the stragglers. Sqn Ldr AS William was awarded Vir Chakra for showing exemplary courage in the face of enemy.

□

In the Northwestern sector, the stocking operations for supplies were mainly carried out by An-12 Squadrons. The aircraft flew round the clock to airlift supplies to Chushul airfield situated at over 14000 ft. Flying there with hardly any navigation aids and landing supplies were feats of airmanship carried out by our pilots and navigators. The supplies to Leh were mainly carried by IL-14 aircraft. The Squadrons flying these aircraft had logged over 1000 hours of flying in November, 1962.

□

Let us leave the bad dream behind and try and look at a few facts with a view to learn some important lessons besides the fact that, when we were facing defeat on all fronts and not a clue what to do about it, the Chinese had declared a ceasefire on November 21, 1962, when they were the master of the situation, and could have stretched their victory trail a lot longer.

Let us not forget that this was not the first debacle of its kind where an Army had been humiliated. We had the Dunkirk during World War II, not forgetting the Japanese lightning campaign in the East, which had left the Allies breathless, and who can forget Pearl Harbour. But unlike the debacles of World War II which have been thoroughly analysed, we have treated the conduct of this war as a holy cow, and refused to analyse it, leave aside discuss it.

I think, we do need to change our concept of patriotism and the security, and grow up a bit, and be mature enough to accept our mistakes, instead of just putting them in the steel vaults—out-of-sight, out-of-mind. It is about time that we had a good look at the Forgotten War.

Some Comments

Field Marshal Cariappa, the first Indian Commander-in-Chief, in his Foreword to Major Ohri's book on NEFA War, writes: "Looking at this matter in all its aspects, I feel main responsibility for this unfortunate setback to our operations in that area could justifiably be laid at the 'political door' and not entirely at the military door. Our army was just a thin green line along the long inhospitable mountainous wooded front, with hardly any depth at all. Our Commanders were ignorant about the enemy's movements. I know there were instances of failures in leadership, but that was not common to our Army alone. Much worse things have happened in other countries in previous wars, but, of course, this is no comfort to us just because similar things have happened elsewhere.

General Thimayya, a former Army Chief, who had set some worthy traditions, was frank and honest in expressing his view, and said: "The reason why we suffered reverses was the lack of a proper coordinated plan. The lack of control over the battle, and our heavy losses of personnel and equipment is the subject matter of an investigation, and I am not qualified or sufficiently informed to make any comments on this part of operations. (*International Studies*, 1963)."

Mr Dutta, in his book, *With Two Presidents*, has aptly quoted President Radhakrishnan: "They came into our house, slapped us, and have gone back." But, then as the Supreme Commander, did President Radhakrishnan order an impartial inquiry into the debacle? The Constitution has vested in the President the ultimate *de jure* powers over the affairs of Armed Forces, yet he did not get the debacle analysed, and had to depend upon the versions of the top brass of the Army, many of whom were the real guilty men of 1962 debacle.

The Government's version itself has distorted the truth. It should have been based on what the Intelligence Bureau and the Army had reported. In the Monograph, *India And The Chinese Invasion*, on page 33 it has been stated, "These vast waves of men were poured against our people and pushed us backwards and backwards, until we were in the last position we were defending. After sometime they surrounded us and that is presumably why it has not been possible to hold position at SELA, which was very very strongly defended, and the Chinese moved to Bomdila."

It would be interesting and useful to find out who gave the above version and why. Obviously, someone was trying to cover-up the facts.

Lt Gen Kaul has misled the government by stating in his request for pre-mature retirement (*The Untold Story*, page 446):

"I said that although our reverses in NEFA were due to the enemy superiority over us in numbers, weapons, logistics, organisation and training, but as they took place at the time I was in command...." That is not true as far as SELA is concerned.

Mankekar in his *Guilty Men Of 1962*, sums up the entire debacle by writing about the Indian Army, "it was outnumbered, out-weaponed, and out-Generalled."

Kuldip Nayyar also mentions about the human wave tactics of the Chinese, and inadequacy of the Indian .303 rifles against automatic weapons of the Chinese.

The facts, of course, are somewhat different. What the Chinese had in the area was about 18,500 troops (11 Div., 55 Div. and 419 Regiment). What we had in the area was 4 Infantry Div. three Brigades, besides the Border Road and Assam Rifles in the area. We had the added advantage of light tanks and

25 pounder guns which the Chinese did not have.

On the balance it was a fair match and we messed it up.

Let us admit that it was a debacle, and the reason for our dismal performance was weak and spineless leadership in the Indian high command. Our General Officer had failed to take timely and decisive measures, and had let the events drift uncontrolled.

It was the worst of times for the Indian Army, a time to hang down our heads in shame. The responsibility lay squarely on the shoulders of high command and their staff. If the fighting had continued beyond November 20, 1962, I feel sure there would have been few left among the ranks who could have effectively directed the Army in war. It was truly a Military Debacle and a Political Disaster.

A Close Hard Look

Now though the Himalayan Blunder is behind us, but the issue is still nagging us. Let us have a close hard look at the problem, because that is first step towards creating some options, and buying peace, even at a price. In a bargain you have to look for the VFM (Value For Money). That is what the world affairs are all about—Give and Take—What you have to weigh up is, how best to minimize your losses and look for the gains that can possibly accrue. It is dangerous to adopt postures in International relations especially if you haven't got the means to enforce your views.

Mr VV Paranjape, a former Joint Secretary in the Ministry of External Affairs, who spent ten years in Beijing, has some views on the Sino-Indian relations which could provide the base for a enduring peace and a meaningful relationship with our Asian neighbour. He has analysed the problem and offers a workable solution as under:

We were *Hindi-Chini Bhai Bhai* till 1956. We had the best of relations and the best of vibes. But then the border dispute erupted in 1958, and soon all the vibes were forgotten and we became enemies. Instead of talking to each other, we started talking at each other, and none too softly.

The border dispute had set in motion a chain reaction which was allowed to spin away uncontrolled. First, it was the verbal war, and this was followed by an armed conflict in 1962, which resulted in a humiliating defeat for us. This was followed by Sino-Pak collaboration. When we look back, this was all because we had a border dispute, and the starting point was our conflicting border claims.

We had claimed that we had an airtight case on our border while the Chinese had no case. China thought otherwise. We had felt that China coveted Indian territory. China said NO to this theory. At this stage we should have realized that there is a solution to every problem as long as you don't make a theory of it.

We strongly felt that we wanted to settle the dispute through negotiations, but it was China which unfairly attacked us without any provocation from our side. We also strongly feel that, thereafter, China has been cultivating Pakistan and has collaborated with it against the interests of India.

NOW. Let us look at the case a bit dispassionately. Even if there is a boundary created by custom, it needs to be ratified by a treaty. We have no treaty with China.

A treaty has to be negotiated and then signed by mutual consent. But we had taken the position that our borders are not negotiable, thereby imposing our version of border on China and blocking all further discussion.

The mistake we made was that we refused to accept that

China also has a view, however, right or wrong. But the very fact that Hindi-Chini held different views, was a clear signal that there is a difference of opinion, and that there did exist a dispute, and that it should be negotiated and settled for good.

We were adamant.

The Chinese Prime Minister came to India in 1960, and put forth a compromise formula on the pattern of Sino-Burmese border treaty, whereby we would retain NEFA area while China would retain Aksai Chin.

We said NO. A FIRM NO.

A word about Aksai Chin. It is a sparsely inhabited tribal area or a no man's land where China or Tibet exercised control. The British had to wrest the control of these areas from Tibet and China, and had met fierce resistance. Pandit Jawaharlal Nehru had aptly described the area as, where not a blade of grass grows, and Indians hardly ever went there.

When we had refused to negotiate, logically we had closed all doors to the peaceful and a mutually agreed settlement. Sadly we had followed this up with the famous Nehru quote, "I have ordered my Generals to throw the Chinese out."

Mao had called the 1962 Conflict as an 'Action in self-defence', which seemed to be the standard Chinese formula when 'Teaching A Lesson', to other countries, be it Vietnam or India. As Khrushchev had pointed out, "India could hardly have initiated the attack when it lost a whole regiment and the war in just two weeks."

The Chinese attack was preplanned as they had warned India of war 15 months earlier—in July, 1961. It is another matter that we were too busy posturing and hardly took any notice of the Chinese threat.

Let me end this with two Chinese quotes which hold the key to Interstate relationships, and I am sure that the Chinese do believe in the old philosophy. The first one is by Confucius:

Kuo Tse Wu Tan Ki

(Don't be afraid to correct a mistake)

And the second one is by Kua T'ien Li Hsia. It tells us about how smallest of gestures can give rise to suspicion. The translation reads as follows:

IN A MELON FARM DON'T TOUCH YOUR SHOES, AND UNDER A PLUM TREE DONOT ADJUST YOUR HEADGEAR.

Rather subtle, but profound and convey a lot. I am sure that you have got the correct message. That is the Chinese style of functioning. The mere grip and the duration of a handshake could tell you the warmth or the coolness with which they are responding. Perhaps, we have yet to learn the Chinese ways.

□

Rajni Kothari in his Foreword to the book, *The Unfought War of 1962: The NEFA Debacle*, puts the whole issue in the correct perspective by raising a few unanswered questions:

- What was Pandit Nehru's own perception about China?
- Was his statement of 1960 that, 'a strong China has always been expansionist,' a sudden revelation of truth, or did he always believe so?
- If he did believe in it, why did he not act earlier?
- Why was the dispute taken from the political to the legal plane in 1959?
- What was the nature of the Soviet advice about Sino-Indian relations? Did it influence decision-making in Delhi.

17

OPERATION DESERT HAWK

Rise and Fall of Ayub Khan

President Ayub Khan was a consummate tactician. "We have," he wrote, "an impeccable enemy in India." Yet he made it known that the essential first step in good neighbourly relations between India and Pakistan would be the settlement of river water dispute. Though not to India's advantage, the Indus Water Treaty was signed by the two countries in September, 1960.

This was a Turning Point.

The line was now clear for the President to attack India at a appropriate time. According to his assessment, India was still weak especially after the defeat by China in 1962. Apart from the Indian morale-in-the-heels, on his side, he was flushed with enormous sophisticated arms aid from America.

After Nehru's death he was emboldened to put through his military plan because his perception of Lal Bahadur Shastri, the new Prime Minister, was not very laudatory. He had, of course, misread that Shastri, a commoner was endowed with uncommon wisdom, and had given a free hand to the Ministry of Defence to forge an effective deterrent to any aggression.

It is small wonder that the Twenty Two Days War, started by Ayub Khan on September 1, 1965 went entirely against his country, forcing him to sign the Tashkent Agreement with India in January 1966, Bhutto, who prided in calling himself a 'confrontation man', hated the transaction and had walked out of Ayub Government to organise a campaign for its downfall. Widespread student disturbance in both Wings of Pakistan had forced Ayub Khan to transfer power to General Yahya Khan on March 25, 1969.

A career that had begun in warm sunshine thus ended in bleak darkness.

Let me begin from the beginning of his end.

Testing Indian Resolve

After the ceasefire in Kashmir in 1949, there had been some minor incidents on the Indo-Pak border and along the ceasefire line in Kashmir, but the tension between the two countries did not burst into a large scale war until April, 1965.

Fighting broke out between the armies of India and Pakistan in the Rann of Kutch, which is a desolate territory and remains under water for half of the year. According to Pakistan, trouble started when on April 4, 1965, Indian Army occupied the Pakistani Post Bing on the pretext that Pakistan had occupied it illegally.

The fact is that Pakistan had put into operation her preplanned 'Operation Desert Hawk', and moved her forces to an area lying between Chad Bet and Beir Bet ostensibly to prevent the Indian Forces from advancing into Pakistani territory. This was followed by a brief battle between India and Pakistan in the Rann of Kutch in which Pakistan had succeeded in pushing back the Indian Forces from the

disputed area.

Pakistan had committed two Infantry Brigades supported by tanks in the disputed area. That was an impressive line-up and our troops had withdrawn from a few posts. We were not quite inclined to commit a large force and make a battle of it in an inhospitable land which hardly had any water supply and road communication with the support bases on our side. We were not trying to play to the gallery. Our plan was to take on the Pakistani challenge if and when required, in a more suitable terrain.

A ceasefire agreement was signed through the mediation of British Prime Minister which provided for restoration of January 1, 1965 position in the Rann of Kutch, and both parties had agreed to submit the dispute to adjudication either through talks or through a three men arbitrational tribunal. The UN Sponsored International Tribunal had favoured Pakistan with 828 sq kms of area in the Rann of Kutch, which was duly honoured by India.

Pakistanis had taken this victory as a major military feat and were convinced that we had yet not recovered from the humiliation of the Himalayan Blunder. Yes. They were right. We were indeed waiting to flex our muscles for a good national cause when and if the need arose.

□

After their Operation Desert Hawk in the Rann of Kutch in April, 1965, President Ayub Khan had made up his mind that it was about time to grab Kashmir by force. This was a major turning point in our military history. We did still have the raw wounds of 1962 festering and the only balm could be a challenge thrown at us, and Ayub Khan provided us with that.

Operation Desert Hawk was a part of the overall plan of Ayub Khan to grab Kashmir by force. He had seen the Indians turn tail, for whatever reasons, in 1962 and the Rann of Kutch was planned to test the Indian resolve. Ayub was more than pleased to see the poor Indian response to his massive onslaught in the Rann of Kutch. He had failed to realize that the lukewarm response by India was by choice because of tactical reasons. But Ayub was so intoxicated with his successes in Rann of Kutch, that he had concluded that it is the right time to strike and he was ready with his next plan.

Old Wine in the Old Bottle

President Ayub Khan had wasted no time in putting into effect the next part of his operational plan, i.e., 'Operation Gibraltar'. It was a repeat performance of the 1947-49 plan. He had pushed in about nine columns of guerrillas into the Kashmir Valley with the fond hope that local population will join hands with the guerrillas and 'PRESTO' he will have Kashmir in his kitty.

The author of this simplistic plan was Major General Akhtar Hussain, GOC No. 12 Infantry Division of Pakistan Army. The Gibraltar Force, about 8000 in number, comprised officers and other ranks of Pakistan Occupied Kashmir Battalion—*Razakars* and *Mujahids*. They were given intensive training in guerrilla warfare schools for six weeks in laying of ambushes, demolishing of bridges and disruption of lines of communication, raids on supply dumps and Unit Headquarters, and armed and unarmed combat. They were supplied with rifles, grenades, shot guns, sten guns, LMGs, 2" and 3" mortars, 83 mm rockets, plastic explosives, wireless sets etc.

Very impressive and very destructive.

It was a repeat trial of the 1947-49 failed plan.

It was the old wine in the old bottle.

The plan was based on three assumptions:

- Wide support would be available across the border.
- India would restrict her operations to PoK territory only.
- There was no possibility of India launching an offensive across the international border.

Wrong

All the three premises proved to be wrong as the Pakistani plan had unfolded itself, and fast slipped down the slope, and ended in a fiasco. The first four Pakistani raiders were captured on August 5, 1965. They didn't have to be persuaded very hard, and had readily spilled the beans about the Pakistani Plan. Thereafter the plan had fallen flat like a damp squib.

Understanding

It is better to understand a little than to misunderstand a lot.

Epigram

He who does not understand your silence, will probably not understand your words.

Elbert Hubbard

Men are apt to believe what they least understand.

Epigram

*President Radhakrishnan with Gen Pathania at Dirang—
"They came into our house, slapped us and have gone back."*

18

OPERATION GRAND SLAM TWENTY TWO DAYS WAR (SEPTEMBER 1 TO 22, 1965)

The Pakistani guerrillas had been infiltrating into Jammu & Kashmir in small batches since late July, 1965 and by the time we had got to know of Pakistani designs in early August, 1965, the guerrillas had been able to set up their bases and strongholds in certain remote areas and some isolated mountain regions which were not easily accessible. They did manage to demolish a number of bridges and culverts; attacked some outposts of Indian Security Forces, and indulged in their normal duties of sabotage, arson and violence in many places, notably Baramula, Badgam, Yusmarg and Srinagar.

The infiltrators did make a nuisance of themselves but beyond that, they were in for a big surprise. Unlike 1947, we didn't need to establish an air bridge and then enlarge the circle of our influence. Then, the raiders had held all the Aces and we had to make do with the Two-of-Clubs but even then we made a fair game of it, the British duplicity notwithstanding. This time we were there and in a short time the tide was turned.

Soon, sooner than Pakistani expectations, the Indian Security Forces had got their act together and started their Operation Bash-Them-Up. They had annihilated about 1000 infiltrators before they realized what hit them, and most of the rest had thought it more prudent to retrace their steps back to where they came from, that is, if they could.

Not only that, the Indian Army decided to go on the offensive, something that the Pakistanis were not quite expecting. It really put the spanner in their works when XV Corps in a swift move captured the important Haji Pir Pass, and the hill feature west of Uri, and were soon threatening Muzzafarabad.

Operation Gibraltar had failed because the bulk of local population didn't oblige the infiltrators by joining them in bringing about an open revolt. The local populace was not quite impressed by the way the so called liberators had gone about making the life of the common man difficult. Moreover, the Army had been quick in sealing the known routes of infiltration thereby denying any reinforcements.

This was a Turning Point in that, the Army had tasted success and carried out some spectacular operations like the Capture of the Haji Pir Pass, and worked to a plan. Nothing succeeds like success.

General Ayub Khan and his boys had done their homework. They were ready with another plan if the Operation Gibraltar flopped, which they did. Seeing the battered and bruised remains of the Operation Gibraltar, they didn't waste any time in putting into motion Operation Grand Slam.

□

The Military Aid received from USA through US-Pak Military Alliance since 1953, and that received from certain other countries, including China, had militarily strengthened Pakistan to a great extent. Pakistan's superiority in modern Tanks (Pattons), better Artillery Equipped with the latest American Guns, Anti-Tank firepower, military aircraft (F-104s), combined with early Warning Radar System, and Microwave Communication Network, and in Naval capability with acquisition of submarines, all this and more, had made President Ayub Khan dream that his American gifted Pattons could easily stroll through the GT Road to conquer Delhi, and had, in fact, planned a tea-party on the ramparts of Red Fort.

In respect of Infantry, taking into consideration the Indian deployments along Indo-China border, in Nagaland, and opposite East Pakistan, The Pakistan Army Strength of 6 Infantry Divisions, and 2 Armoured Divisions in West, was not inferior to Infantry Divisions of India, some of which were under-strength and newly raised, and the three Brigades of Armour deployed in the West. In several crucial terms, Pakistan was superior to India qualitatively, and in numerical strength deployed against each other, the two countries were more or less equal.

The Pakistani Military Leaders had provided that if 'Operation Gibraltar' met with any serious problems, 'Operation Grand Slam' would be put into effect.

□

In a quick move by Pakistan on September 1, 1965, after a heavy shelling by heavy and medium artillery and mortars on all the Indian forward posts along the Cease Fire Line (CFL) especially in Chhamb-Mandiala Area, from 3.30 am to 6.30 am, one Squadron of Patton Tanks carrying Infantry had crossed the International border between Burejal and Pussa.

The Pakistani objective was to cut off the Jammu-Srinagar highway at Akhnur. It was a determined move by Pakistan with a lot of dust kicked up and the fireworks. Here they had caught us not quite prepared to meet and match up to the Pakistani offensive. It sent us reeling, and soon the Army was in a desperate situation as our own armour was still a couple of days away from the scene of action, and it would have been unrealistic to expect Pakistan to wait for the arrival of our tanks to make a match of it.

The Pakistani Armour was on the roll and there appeared to be little to stop them in their tracks and save Akhnur and thereby the all important Jammu-Srinagar highway. The solitary Indian Brigade in the area was in no position to make a fight of it. His fight was for survival right from the word go. The Brigade Commander had been asking for the air support because that was the only plausible saviour under the circumstances.

It is at this late stage when the Pakistani Armour was just a whisper away from their objective and the solitary Indian Brigade in the area was facing virtual annihilation, that the Army Chief General JN Choudhuri had realized that he was at the end of his rope and the only possible knot he could tie at the end of the rope to hang on for life, was a quick response by the Air Force to stop the advancing Pakistani columns and give him some breathing time to get his act together.

Air Chief Remembers

Air Chief Marshal Arjan Singh, DFC, (Retd), in his

Foreword to one of my earlier books *Profiles Of Courage* (1992), reminisced about the Air war in 1965, "The Defence Apparatus of the country has been a sacred cow. Debate on various aspects of security has been discouraged in Parliament and amongst the public. This has, in a way, resulted in the inadequacy of planning and proper equipment. There has been much adhocism and reaction to events rather than a long term plan. This is partly due to lack of strategic intelligence and assessment of future threats.

The 1965 War with Pakistan brought out our weakness in this respect. Despite intrusions by Pakistan into J&K by its regulars as *Mujahidins* etc., we did not clearly foresee that Pakistan may attack in strength. We were unable to assess that attack may be launched with a view to cutting off our links of communication to Poonch and to Kashmir Valley. The attack on Chhamb-Jaurian Sector on September 1, 1965, was a surprise and swift in execution. We were falling back to an Armour Attack and Akhnur Bridge was in danger.

It was under this situation that General Chaudhuri asked me for Air Support. We both went to Defence Minister, YB Chavan, and asked for clearance for air attack. That was given instantly. It was late in the afternoon and Air Force had to be quick to be effective. All the aircraft available at Pathankot were airborne within an hour and attacked the invading force. While the results achieved cannot be assessed accurately, but one fact is known; Pak forces did not advance beyond the area where they were attacked.

In 1965, PAF had a tremendous reputation built up by American publicity machine and its aircraft—Sabres and F-104s—donated to Pakistan. As more often than not, we had under-assessed our own capabilities, the result was that we were unduly cautious in air operations. However, as the war proceeded, we established our faith in our own aircraft, particularly in Gnats, and were able to attack all targets up to Peshawar, Quetta and Karachi with Canberra aircraft.

Our fighters—Hunters, Mysteres—attacked trains, convoys and army formations behind the fighting area; they also supported the Army in the fighting area as jointly decided by the two services. Sargodha, a highly defended airbase was attacked many a time with reasonable results. The PAF attack on Pathankot was successful, but their attacks on Halwara, Ambala and Adampur were utter failure with many losses of PAF aircraft, and caused no damage whatsoever at the base."

□

Pakistan Moves on a Confident Note

Pakistan had opened its innings on a very confident note and as hot favourite in the early hours of September 1, 1965. It had announced its none too honest intentions with an artillery barrage across the ceasefire line in Chhamb-Jaurian Sector in Kashmir.

Pakistani Planners had obviously done their homework, and had planned their offensive meticulously. This Sector, as rightly concluded by the Pakistani Planners, was our Achilles' Heel. Pakistan held all the Aces and the chances of success. 'Hundred Percent', they had thumped the table and with good justification.

First, they had the initial advantage of time and place, being the one to make the opening move. Then, they had the terrain fully in their favour with a super-highway drive-in right from their cantonment to the battle area. They, of course, had excellent intelligence system, and knew about our total lack of heavy armour in this Sector.

And, you can't forget their morale. They were raring and straining at the leash. They had the satisfaction of seeing the Indian Army on-the-run in 1962, and the restraint displayed by us in the Kutch Episode in April, 1965, had made them conclude it as a reluctance on the part of the Indian Army to face the brave Pakistani soldiers.

Add to it the fact that the Pakistani Planners had thrown-in one Infantry Division, and two Tank Regiments (70-90 tanks), and facing this massive force on-the-roll was one Infantry Brigade on the Indian side with, of course, no heavy armour support. And the Pakistanis knew this.

Where would you bet your money?

No doubt, Pakistan held a winning hand.

In the Pakistan GHQ, the Planners had the satisfaction of seeing their plan unfold as per schedule. They saw their Columns rolling Eastwards and heading for a skirmish with the Indian Infantry Brigade which, they were confident, would be overrun by the two tank regiments before the end of the day.

Back home in New Delhi, as the Indian Strategists had looked at the Situation Map, they were alarmed at how right the Pakistani Planners were. There was nothing to stop the Pakistani onslaught in the Chhamb Sector. Our Infantry Brigade was not expected to last till the evening in view of the intensity of the invading force. Our own Armour which could contend with the thrust was still a couple of driving days away.

That was bad news.

BUT PAKISTANI THRUST HAD TO BE STOPPED AT ALL COSTS.

□

The Crucial Moments

'WITHIN AN HOUR'

Air Marshal Arjan Singh, Chief of the Air Staff, had unhesitatingly replied when the Defence Minister, on request from the Chief of the Army Staff, had queried, "How soon the IAF can render support to our Army in the Chhamb sector?"

The date was September 1, 1965; Time: 1600 Hrs;

Place: South Block, New Delhi.

There was a visible relief on the faces of the gathering at the emergency meeting to discuss the latest war situation which, understandably, was less than satisfactory, because Pakistan had the choice of time and place to launch the attack on India, and thus the initial advantage till the drama unfolded and gathered the Indian response.

□

IAF Responds

Air Marshal Raja Ram, DFC, AOC-in-C, Western Air Command, IAF had got the 'Code Word' on September 1, 1965, in the late afternoon. The whole machinery was put into operation down the line at our air bases. There was feverish activity. The pilots had to be briefed, the aircraft suitably armed for the respective missions for a multi-pronged attack emanating from different air bases.

Time was of prime importance. We had no night flying capability and the next hour or so was crucial, because on this hung the fate of the Indian Infantry Brigade.

The Indian Brigade Commander had been told that Air Support was on the way, and that he was to fight a holding battle.

'BUT FOR HOW LONG?', the Brigade Commander had

wondered. His troops were already in contact and the battle had commenced. He needed the Air Support *Ek Dam Jaldi*.

The Pakistani Brigade and the Tank Regiment was full of zest, and dictating and calling the shots. It was quite a hammering that the Indians had to accept, because they had no answer to the Pakistani Armour thrust. The minutes were ticking away and the Indian Brigade Commander was understandably a worried man as he saw the sun inching towards the western horizon. He hated the prospect of a night battle with his available resources. His ears longed to hear the roar of the Indian Jets, and he kept straining his eyes scanning the horizon in the South from where he hoped his help would emerge.

□

It was precisely at 1719 hrs (5.19 pm), according to the ATC Log maintained at our forward air base, that the Falcon Formation, comprising four Vampires operating in pairs had got airborne.

The destination was in Chhamb Sector.

Their briefing was crisp and laconic.

'BASH 'EM UP'.

As the Vampires had reached the battle zone, the pilots had seen an array of Pakistani tanks and vehicles. They seemed to be everywhere.

The Indian Brigade Commander was overjoyed.

The Pakistani Brigade Commander was a bit surprised when he saw the aircraft, but had reassuringly concluded that they must be the Reconnaissance planes. Surely, the Indians are not going to commit their Air Force. It wasn't a part of his briefing or calculations.

The two lead Vampires had turned-in line-astern for the

attack and commenced the dive. The Pakistani Commander was dazed. He had ordered his Ack-Ack guns to open up as the Vampires had continued with their dive for the attack.

The Falcons had the Pakistani Armour right and proper on their gun sights. It was a BLOODY battle between 1719 (5.19 pm) and 1905 (7.05 pm) i.e., precisely one hour and forty one minutes. The Indian Air Force had launched and carried out twenty-six sorties over the battle area, relentlessly attacking the enemy tanks and giving them no respite.

The honour and distinction of opening the Indian Air Account goes to the Vampires and Mysteres of 3, 31, and 45 Squadrons. When the Indian Fighter Pilots had called it a day, they had left behind a totally bewildered invading force, gathering its debris and regrouping.

The confirmed tally for the evening was thirteen tanks, sixty-two vehicles, two guns and unspecified casualties in troops.

A VERY SATISFYING EVENING, ALL SAID AND DONE.

Another interesting aspect of this recorded history is the fact that while the IAF swung into action within an hour, it took two days for the PAF before they made their appearance in this Sector on September 3, 1965.

'Within An Hour' are not only the finest words and the hour for the IAF but a maxim which depicts the mobility, flexibility and ability of the Air Force to concentrate their fire-power 'Where-Action-Is'.

Tango Remembers

Flight Lieutenant (later Air Marshal) Tarlochan Singh (Tango), PVSM, AVSM, VrC, VM, remembers that exciting evening when he had gone in for the attack in Chhamb Sector on the opening day.

"It was September 1, 1965. The area was Chhamb in the western sector. We had been playing the waiting game at the ORP (Operational Readiness Platform). The Ground Liaison Officer (GLO) had briefed us. The intelligence had been accurate and we knew precisely where the breakthrough had taken place. The things were pretty grim in fact. The Pakistani tanks had crossed over and were merrily cruising along with practically nil opposition on the ground.

I was in a Mystere Squadron. We were four of us. The Mystere is literally a flying armoury. It carried thirty eight 68 mm Rockets and another 55 in the belly, besides two deadly DECCA Cannons of 30 mm calibre. That is a lot of punch. It was a deadly flying platform against anything on the ground. In the air combat, it is not too bad, but we had the Gnats to give us air cover, and keep our tails clear while we concentrated on the ground targets.

We had got the word around sunset. I can't forget the sight. As we had reached the Sector, it was already dusk. But we were overjoyed as we had approached the target area. You had to see it to believe it—THERE WERE TANKS AND MORE TANKS, IN SHORT, TANKS GALORE. They had no camouflage even. It is hard to believe, but it is true.

NEXT?

We literally ran amuk, or the tanks did. It was 'BANG, BANG, BANG', all the way.

It was a glorious sight. We had drawn the first blood and had felt sorry when no ammo was left, because we knew that we couldn't get another mission on that day because it was already getting dark, and the next mission will have to wait till the next day.

But as we were heading back home after the attack, it gladdened our hearts to see another two formations of Mysteres heading for the sector to continue with the Patton-bashing. The Pakistani tanks had quite a bashing that they least expected, nor were they quite prepared, for, so far, they had been merrily cruising along unopposed into the Indian territory.

Too bad for them, but they had asked for it. But I guess, we gave our OGs (Olive Greens as the Air Force fondly calls the Army Jawans because of the colour of their uniform) the much needed breath to gather up their tools, get their bearings right, and get on with the good job where we had left off.

Since this was the first operational mission—The Real Thing—there was a lot of excitement when we had landed back after a highly successful mission. I remember the first word I had uttered as I entered the crew room that late evening was *TABLA BAJA DIA* (Bashed The Hell Out Of Them). But it was a difficult night to pass because all the boys were keyed up to have a go at the 'Pakistani Tanks' next morning.

And, of course, the next morning we had painted it red—literally. We used to go really low as Mysteres were ideal for low flying with the cockpit right in front, which enabled the pilot to see almost below his nose. The open skies were left for the Tiny Gnats—which justifiably earned for themselves the name of 'Sabre Bashers'.

Soon a stage had come when the sight of a Mystere formation approaching the battle area over Chhamb used to spread panic amongst the Patton Tank crews, who could be seen jumping out and running as we used to set the sights and let go the rockets. Perhaps, like the Gnats, the Mysteres could truly be called the Patton Bashers.

Looking back at that point of time, there was nothing to stop the Pakistani tanks from merrily driving along on their victory run. It was, perhaps, this very air attack in the dying moments of the first day of the Twenty Two Days War, which changed the course of the battle."

Battle Areas to Airbases

The first attack on the Indian air bases close to western border was launched on September 6, 1965, by Pakistan Air Force in the afternoon at about 5 pm. The targets were Adampur and Halwara by the PAF fighters based at Sargodha; Pathankot and Srinagar by the fighters based at Peshawar; and Jamnagar from Karachi. Some of our radar installations such as those at Ferozepur in Punjab and Porbander in Gujarat were also attacked.

The PAF Sabres heading for Adampur were intercepted by four Hunters; the mission did not succeed. At Halwara also, the Hunters took on the Sabres and the PAF had a bad day losing three in the now famous and an exciting Air Battle Over Halwara. At Pathankot, the PAF had a fairly satisfying visit, as they managed to damage a few aircraft on ground.

Retaliating to the first enemy air raid, in the morning of September 7, 1965, at 0530 am, the IAF had returned the PAF compliment of their uninvited visits the previous evening. Six Mysteres had raided Sargodha, the most important airbase in Pakistan which was considered to be virtually impregnable by the PAF Planners.

One Star Fighter (F-104) was scrambled by PAF and had shot down one of our Mysteres without much effort and reasonable ease, because the Mystere were basically a ground attack aircraft, in fact, it was called a 'Flying Armoury' because of the lethal load it could carry, the asset which made it quite unsuitable for a dog fight, that too with a F-104, one of the best air defence fighters of its time. But the score was soon evened out when another Mystere had got on the tail of the F-104 and shot it down over their own home base. It was quite an achievement considering the relative merits of the Mysteres *Vs* F-104s. We had carried out four raids on Sargodha that day.

The same morning Barrackpore, Bagdogra and Kalaikunda, were raided by PAF twice with their fighters based in East Pakistan. This was quite unexpected as we had no intention of escalating the conflict to the Eastern Sector. But Pakistan had thought otherwise, and were able to inflict some losses on the ground during their first raid which had caught us quite unprepared and by surprise. We had paid the price for not expecting the unexpected, which is quite a done thing in war i.e., to do what the other side does not expect you to do.

But in their second raid, the PAF was not quite so lucky as we had learnt our lesson fast and proper, and the PAF lost two Sabres over Kalaikunda—a price they paid for underestimating their adversary. Not quite a done thing in war.

Pakistan had very substantial anti-aircraft protection at their important airfields such as Sargodha, Mauripur, Peshawar, as well as their radar signal unit at Sakesar and Badin. We did manage to bomb their airfields at Sargodha, Risalwala, Chak Jhumra, Multan, Nawabshah, Peshawar and Kohat. In our bomber raids we had lost only one Canberra Bomber to ground fire over Sargodha on September 21, 1965.

September 7, 1965, was a very very busy day for both the Air Forces—IAF as well as PAF. On this day maximum

number of air raids on each other's airfields with formations of fighters were carried out. Obviously, both the Air Forces were trying hard to get a favourable air situation. There were some losses on both the sides. After this, both the PAF and IAF had cut back on the day-light raids on the air bases because they were proving to be rather expensive and with diminishing returns. Idea is not to play to the gallery but to try and see if the damage caused by such raids is worth the risks taken. It wasn't.

On 13/14 night our Canberra Bombers had raided another bastion of PAF—Peshawar airbase which is also the Headquarters of PAF. It was at the extreme range of our Bombers, but they had a fruitful raid, and was effective enough to make the PAF remove a part of the PAF Bomber force to Risalpur airbase.

Another interesting aspect of the Air War-1965 has been that, eventhough both the sides had delivered a fairly large tonnage of bombs on each other, but unluckily some, if not many of the bombs had failed to explode—they were old and had been supplied to the two Air Forces mostly by the same source.

Our Signal Unit at Amritsar, code-named 'Fish Oil' by Pakistan, invited a lot of attention from PAF. It was honoured with daily visits, morning and evening, by an increasing number of Sabres escorted by F-104s and finally accompanied by Canberras on the morning and evening sorties of September 12, 1965.

The aggression in Kashmir had been stopped successfully by us. Pakistan had changed the Command of their forces in the Chhamb Sector from General Akhtar Hussain Malik, who had planned and initiated this operation, to General Yahya

Khan. 'Changing horses mid-stream', as Air Marshal Asghar Khan put it.

One aspect of the Pakistan plan remains puzzling. On the first night when the fighting began, the PAF para-dropped from their C-130s a handful of Commando Forces on the three forward air bases at Pathankot, Adampur and Halwara, at about 2 am. That was a badly planned futile effort. In the Pathankot area about sixty men were dropped. They landed amid a network of canals and were unable to rendezvous. Pathankot is scarcely ten miles from the border, but only about ten of these men managed to return to Pakistan, the rest were apprehended. At Halwara and Adampur, some of the soldiers landed in the residential areas, and some in the surrounding sugarcane fields, and were caught by the villagers and handed over to the police or military. What this futile operation aimed to achieve is difficult to understand.

□

Ayub Khan was a worried man. On September 22, 1965, at the UN Security Council, ZA Bhutto had ranted, "We will wage a war for thousand years." Yet on September 23, 1965, the very next day, the ceasefire was declared. Ayub Khan is said to have dispensed with the services of about a dozen Generals and forty or so Brigadiers and Colonels.

SOME EXCITING AIR BATTLES

September, 1965 War

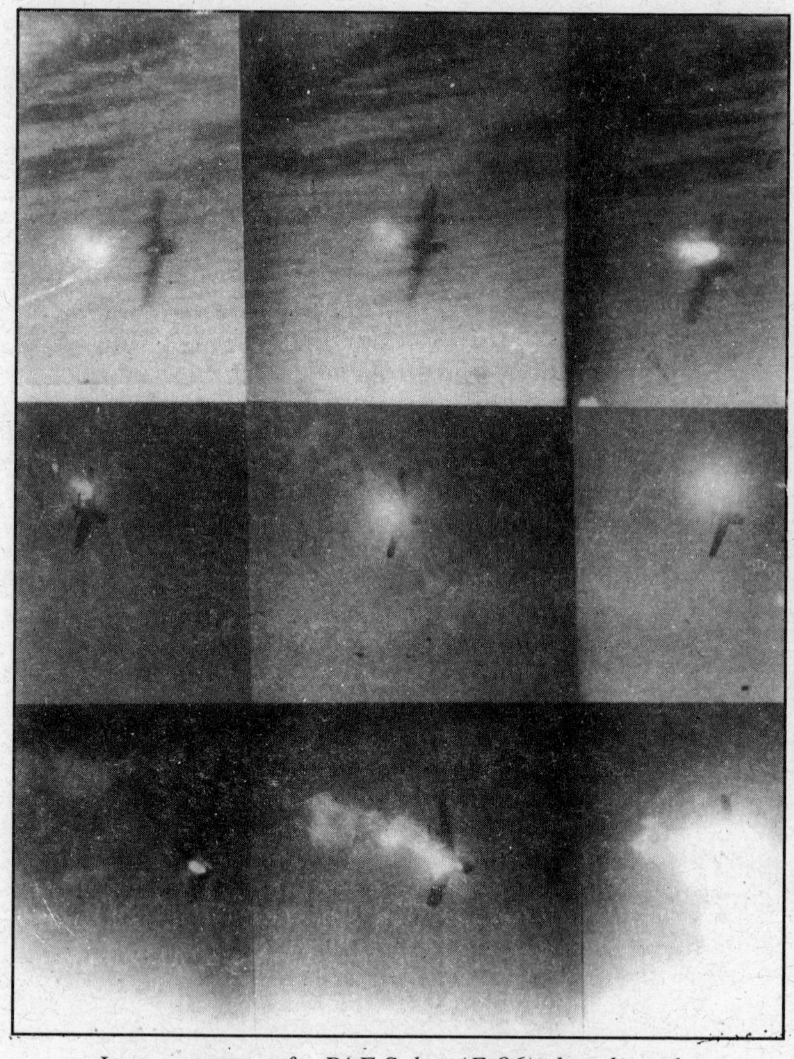

Last moments of a PAF Sabre (F-86) shot down by Gnats during 1965 operations.

19

OUR FIRST AIR KILL

As Recorded By Panthers

"The September 3, 1965, was a historic day for the Air Force and No. 23 Squadron—The Panthers—and personally for Squadron Leader Trevor Keelor. It was on this day that, the First Ever Air Battle in the history of Indian Air Force was fought with The Panthers bagging the honours and Trevor claiming the First-Ever Air-Kill for the IAF in this air battle.

This air battle took place in the Akhnur Sector when two Mystere fighter bombers of IAF, acting as a decoy, showed themselves in the area, attacked the enemy positions on the ground, and headed home at tree-top level, leaving the Four aircraft Gnat Formation there to suitably deal with the F-86s and F-104s of Pakistan Air Force (PAF).

In brief, the tactics used by the two Gnat Formations was to have the Lead Offensive Four to do a tight spiral up over the area in a Combat Patrol Formation, followed 3000 feet lower and 1000 feet behind by the Second Defensive Four led by Trevor Keelor in Tactical Formation. It was an improvised manoeuvre not quite the classical copybook type.

The initial encounter took place at 20,000 feet when one

over-keen F-86 in his excitement to latch on to the lead Gnat in the Front Four made a nice piece of cheese in a fine sandwich that gave him the great honour of being the first F-86 to be downed in an air combat. His next interest in this fight must have been only on the following day when he must have read about it in *DAWN*, or was it *The Pakistan Times*, that is, if he was still kicking and had not locked in with Saint Peter."

In Trevor's Own Words

"We decided we should have an Offensive Defensive Formation. When we went into the area, we flew at a very low level and we immediately eased up so that their radar could pick us up. They (PAF Radar) did, and they (PAF Fighters) came. That was the whole idea.

We carried out some tactical manoeuvres. Sure enough it foxed them. One came right up to my side eventually. He was sandwiched between the lead formation and mine at the rear. We shot it out of the sky.

He had (I could see as I was closing-in), two Side-Winder Air-to-Air missiles 'On' and I was a little out of range at that time. So I just moved my throttle forward. We have a wonderful acceleration, and I cosed-in very quickly.

I sighted him, and in my very first burst the right side of his aircraft disintegrated and he went flicking over his back absolutely out of control, and that is why he went down."

20

AIR BATTLE OVER HALWARA

There Were Four of Them

Four Sabre Jets (F-86s) of Pakistan Air Force (PAF) had come screaming low across the border over the plains of Punjab at tree-top level, thus successfully dodging our radar and the watchful eyes.

Their aim was, "To Bash-up Our Forward Air Base At Halwara in the Northern Sector."

And, what is more, they were suitably armed for their mission with Rockets and Front Guns which had the potential to create enough mess at the airfield, and keep us busy and worried for quite sometime.

The date was September 6, 1965, the initial stages of the Twenty Two Days War when both sides were testing and teasing each other to establish areas of Air Superiority, and also give maximum possible help to own ground troops to carry out their respective plans.

The time was forty minutes past six in the evening, and the western horizon was aglow with the setting September Sun.

Admittedly, the PAF had been amply successful in the

first phase of their attack on Halwara, that is, they had been able to reach one of our bastions undetected.

The four Pakistani Sabres had pulled up for some sharp shooting and attacking selective targets at Halwara airbase, and there appeared to be little to stop the PAF fighter pilots from achieving their aims, and going back across the border to file in their Mission Reports to say,

"Mission Completed."

At that point of time it so happened that, the euphoria of the PAF fighter pilots was shared, to a large extent, in the form of apprehensions by many down at the airbase that soon they are going to be subjected to some solid fireworks by the PAF F-86s because, there appeared to be nothing to stop them or counter them.

The PAF pilots had given practically no reaction time to get our act together. And that meant a lot of trouble.

But

As often happens, there is always a scope for a counter-surprise in war, and it has been rightly said that: "You have not won, till you HAVE."

The PAF fighters still had many seconds to go before they could be qualified to write in their Authorisation Books back in their Squadron—DCO (Duty Carried Out).

There was an unpleasant surprise for the Pakistani pilots just a few moments ahead for which they were not quite prepared.

What was not known to the PAF Formation was the fact that, at that point of time Four Hunter Fighter Bombers were carrying out a Combat Air Patrol (CAP) over Halwara airbase and that, soon, sooner than later, they will be there to put the spanner in the Pakistani fireworks.

The first section of the Indian Hunter Fighter aircraft was led by Flight Lieutenant Pingle with Flying Officer Gandhi as his No. 2, and the second section was led by Flight Lieutenant Rathore, with Flying Officer Neb as his No. 2.

Now

There were four Hunters *vs* four Sabres.

That sounded a lot healthier and nice, and the stage was set for an interesting Air Battle over Halwara, where no quarters can be asked for or given.

In an Air Battle the rules of the game are pretty stiff, unbending, ruthless but simple:

"He Who Shoots First And Right,WINS."

As simple as that.

Your past laurels have little relevance beyond giving you the potential to win, but in the final analysis, what matters and decides the Winner is your performance at that point of time that confers the right to live or die.

The Air Scenario

There was no prior warning about the imminent air attack on Halwara airbase, and to that extent the PAF had been able to achieve total surprise, a big winning factor considering the fact that in an air attack you work in terms of seconds, and that hardly gives you the luxury of some sort of reaction time.

As the PAF formation had pulled up for their attack on the Halwara airbase, one Section of our Hunter Fighters led by Flight Lieutenant Pingle and Flying Officer Gandhi as his No. 2 was on the down wind of the runway at Halwara. Flight Lieutenant Rathore and Flying Officer Neb were about fives miles away from the airbase.

The PAF leader of the formation who was almost ready for his attack on the Halwara airbase, was the first to spot the two Hunter fighters on the down wind leg.

By the time Flight Lieutenant Pingle and Flying Officer Gandhi had spotted the four Sabres, it was a split second too late, and they were totally surprised by the presence of the uninvited guests over our skies.

On the ground, by now, Air Raid siren had been sounded, and the ground defences alerted about the imminent air attack. Our Air Defence Gunners, always on the alert, were setting the correct elevation on their guns to get their sights right and proper on the enemy aircraft.

With this scenario, what followed was a spine-chilling Air Battle over Halwara airbase; an Air Battle in which, admittedly, the PAF had an edge over us because of the initial total surprise that they had been able to achieve by reaching Halwara undetected right till the time they had pulled up for their attack.

The Air Battle

Flying Officer Gandhi had seen the Leader of the PAF Formation getting behind Flight Lieutenant Pingle's aircraft, and had shouted on his R/T as a reflex action:

"Pingles Sabre behind you. Watch out."

It was too late.

Flying Officer Gandhi had seen a burst of angry fire from the PAF Leader's Sabre jet which had Pingles right and proper in his gun-sight.

There was a flash and a cloud of smoke, and the next moment Pingle's Hunter aircraft was in a steep dive, B-U-R-N-I-N-G.

The very next moment Gandhi was relieved to see tiny canopy separating, and Pingle bailing out to safety from the burning Hunter aircraft.

Score Settled

At that very moment, the PAF Leader in his enthusiasm had overshot Gandhi and came right in front of him, and all that Flying Officer Gandhi had to say was a big , 'THANK YOU', followed by a minor correction to get the PAF Leader in the centre of his gun-sight, and then do what comes naturally to a fighter pilot and gives him the greatest joyous moment of his life:

"Rat - A - Tat - Tat."

Gandhi made no mistake about it.

A short burst from his front gun was all that was required to settle the score with PAF.

"Pingles this is for you; no debts with PAF," Gandhi had whispered to himself.

But

He did not know or realize that No. 2 of the PAF Leader was on his tail to settle the score for the PAF, and by the time Gandhi had got warning to take any evasive action, it was too late.

The Pakistani fighter pilot had closed-in behind Gandhi's Hunter, and given a short burst from his front gun which had set Gandhi's aircraft aflame.

It was Gandhi's turn to bail out and join his Leader Pingle on the ground minus their Hunters. The Score was 1:2, with PAF leading.

The Battle Goes On

Our Ack-Ack Guns had been following the No. 2 of PAF formation, and as soon as the Sabre had broken off after shooting down Gandhi, our Gunners had their settings right.

"F - 1 - R - E," the Air Defence Regiment Commander had ordered.

It was a direct hit.

The familiar flash; a cloud of smoke; a ball of fire; and the Sabre jet was no more.

There was a BIG Hurrah on the ground with the usual: *Woh Mara.*

The score was 2:2.

Rathore Joins the Battle

Flight Lieutenant Rathore and Flying Officer Neb had spotted the PAF Formation when the Air Battle over Halwara was already 'On' with the PAF Leader having got behind Pingle's tail.

Rathore had immediately turned towards the airbase together with Neb to join the Air Battle. They had seen two Hunters and two Sabres shot down in quick succession.

Now

It was their turn and up to them to improve upon the score. Happily, this time it was the turn of the Pakistani pilots to be surprised. They were not aware about Rathore and Neb being in the vicinity of the airfield.

The remaining two Sabres were in no further mood to engage in any kind of air combat. They had descended low and headed West into the setting sun to get across the border and back to their home base with some unhappy tales to tell.

Although Rathore and Neb had kept a sharp eye on the two fleeing Sabres but for a moment they had lost contact as the PAF fighters were, understandably, flying really low, and Rathore and Neb had the sun in their eyes.

Nevertheless, our two Hunters had continued with the chase hoping to make contact soon enough before they get across the border.

Then

Rathore got the break he was looking for. The two PAF fighters had made the fatal mistake of strafing the ground to get rid of the ammunition, and kicked up some puffs of dust.

Rathore, with all his fighter experience behind him, had no difficulty in spotting the Sabres from the tell-tale dust puffs.

Rathore had given a burst of throttle to catch up with the Sabres, and was soon behind to take a potshot.

At about 1000 yards Rathore had got behind the Sabre on the right and asked Neb to take on the Sabre on the left.

Rathore closed-in to about 500 yards, and gave a burst from his front guns.

The Sabre started banking to the left, and then nosedived into the ground, exploding into a huge sheet of fire and flame, some five or six miles from the airbase.

Neb had closed-in further behind the second PAF Sabre and fired a burst from about 400 yards. Neb closed-in further to about 100 yards and fired again on the sharply climbing Sabre which presented a much better target.

Neb saw pieces flying off the Sabre as his cannon shells had found their mark on the left wing.

There was first a puff of smoke which rapidly turned into a sheet of flame as the last of the PAF Sabre fighters formation of Four had disintegrated in mid-air.

The whole drama, according to the ATC Log Book, took about six minutes.

It was an expensive misadventure attempted by PAF.

With the Squadron pilots during a mess function at one of our fighter air bases.

21

THE BURNING TRAIN

Oh! To Be A Fighter Pilot

The most cherished dream of a fighter pilot is to command a fighter outfit someday and, I too had such a dream. The fantasy around which the young fighter pilot weaves his imagination while being introduced to the adventure, excitement and ideals of flying, is the dream of engaging the enemy in an aerial combat and defeating him in the sky.

You pick him up before he does far away in the sky where he gives away his position with a glint of sunlight reflected from his streaking aircraft. Your eyes find and stay glued to him, lest you lose sight of him. Oh! nerves go tense, blood rushes, and you feel your heart pounding as the distance between you two closes.

At this stage it would have been ideal to close-in stealthily behind him, set gun-sight squarely in the middle of his cockpit—1000 yards—800 yards—approaching the firing range; enemy aircraft growing bigger and bigger, when you can almost see the eye-balls of the adversary, and with a gaiety press the trigger. TUT-TUT-TUT of the four blasting guns shake your aircraft and tingle your being to its core. You simultaneously see metal chinks flying off the body of the enemy aircraft; then a thin line of smoke emerges followed soon by the flames leaping from the wings and the engine of the aircraft.

The enemy aircraft goes crazy, it pitches up in the sky, nose drops violently and starts spinning like a top, heading back for the ultimate meeting with the Mother Earth. Our budding fighter does not want to open his eyes as yet, and in his imagination continues to follow the doomed quarry till the moment of ultimate delight.

That is: To see the mighty flash of light and mushrooming of a huge column of black smoke, announcing the occurrence of the inevitable impact of the crash and the final fulfilment of his sacred mission.

The Burning Train

The role of the Air force is, firstly, to provide Air Defence of our own vital areas and points; secondly, to attack and destroy the enemy Air Force to stop it from interfering with our ground and air operations; thirdly, to attack and destroy the enemy's potential i.e., industrial, economic, logistics etc., to wage a war against us; fourthly, to support the Army's ground operations in the immediate battlefield by attacking enemy targets which are beyond the range of artillery guns; and fifthly, to interdict lines of communications such as railways, rolling stocks, railway yards, roads, bridges, and enemy's armour supply, storage dumps of fuel and ammunition behind the enemy lines.

□

On September 8, 1965, I was asked to undertake a

Mission to support our army in the battlefield in the Lahore-Kasur Sector, where they were being pushed very hard by the Pakistani armour thrust. Their tanks were threatening to advance against a very determined resistance by the Indian armour.

I Bhoop, BK Bishnoi, later Air Vice Marshal was No. 4 in the formation which was led by Flight Lieutenant CKK Menon, Flight Lieutenant AS Khullar was No. 2, and Flight Lieutenant DS Nagi was the sub-section leader and No. 3. Our task was to locate and destroy enemy tanks, and attack supply lines supporting them.

I was very excited at the thought of first time crossing into Pakistani territory for a real encounter for which I had hitherto practiced in simulated training exercises when dummy tanks did not fire back at me.

It was going to be a lifetime experience not only to be remembered but narrated to my generations. I had prayed:

"O God give me the courage that I can live up to the expectations."

Little nervousness, a little anxiety, a little apprehension of the unknown came and passed as we got down to collect the target information, preparing the maps, route and briefing. This took us about an hour.

We got airborne and headed for the first turning point. To remain undetected by the enemy radar, we had to fly low. We were skimming the trees, barely thirty feet above the ground in a broad frontage. Clocking speed of 420 knots, the ground passed so fast that the features looked blurred.

I suddenly saw a huge canal pass below me. I searched the map but there was no canal marked on the map! It confused me, where was I?

"What was that?" I asked the leader.

"Who knows," he responded.

(We later learnt that it was the famous Ichhogal Canal which was not marked on our maps and had been built as a major obstacle for an Indian attack.)

However, we pressed on as per our flight plan, and reached the designated target. Till that time we maintained R/T silence. Suddenly, the silence was broken with a crisp short call from the leader:

"Switches On."

"Three and Four step back, look for tanks."

We spread out in a loose formation and had hoped that we would see a huge congregation of tanks milling around the area. But we saw none. Some stray vehicles were seen moving on the road, but no trace of the tanks.

While searching the area for the Pakistani tanks we reached Raiwind Railway Station, and to our amazement, we saw a very long train steaming-in. Its open wagons were loaded with heavy tanks, armoured cars, and the closed wagons heading for the battle zone, presumably carried fuel and ammunition for tanks.

That was a prize catch, and all by a stroke of luck.

Leader promptly called off the search for the moving tanks, and in lieu targeted the train. We spread out along the length of the train, dividing it equally in four fair and equal parts. I, being No. 4, was at the end of the attacking formation.

I saw the Leader unleash a salvo of his T-10 rockets which struck the wagons close to the engine. There was a flash of light, and then a chain of explosions blasting a number of wagons.

Similarly, I watched the rockets of No. 2 and 3 score

direct hits on some open and some close wagons which jumped into the 'Air'as they exploded belching fire and thick black smoke.

I was so thrilled watching the fireworks that I failed to observe that my aircraft was engulfed with black and white smoke puffs. O'hell! they were the anti-aircraft Ack-Ack shells bursting. Never thought they could weave such beautiful patterns. I laid my gunsight on the remaining last quarter of the ill-fated train and let go my rockets. There was a brief call on the R/T from the Leader:

"Good Show Bhoop! Direct Hits!"

The natter had continued:

"Let us have another bash at them. I think some rockets are still left."

"Roger 2."

"Roger 3."

"Roger 4. I think I am hit, but the aircraft is behaving. Following you."

We went in for the second attack, demolishing whatever was left of the train, or the area of the railway station around. There was a raging inferno of fire and huge columns of thick black smoke.

It was incredible and a sight to behold!

En route to the base we found a column of Pakistani lorries and armoured cars heading for the Indian border. We engaged them with guns and had a field day. I knocked out atleast five of them, and the formation left a large number of them upturned and burning on the roadside.

A tremendous experience. After landing, my aircraft was found with 36 holes made by the enemy Ack-Ack. A mission well accomplished and a part of my ambition and desire to take part and test my skills someday in actual war, met.

I was initiated.

The above mission was nothing much to write home about. It was only after a 'Call' came from Headquarters at Delhi congratulating the Squadron and narrating the effect of the strike on the course of the war, that we grasped its impact.

The Pakistani tanks pushing against our armour were on the verge of exhausting their fuel and ammunition stocks. To supplement that and maintain the momentum of this thrust, this train was carrying huge stocks and additional tanks for the next morning's operations.

The denial of this vital supply was a major factor causing the enemy to withdraw its armour from the sector with heavy losses.

Mission: Patton Bashing

Next morning, the September 8, 1965, the Pakistani tanks in Khemkaran Sector were on the move with the intention of reaching in a non-stop mode. Their government had made no secret of their intentions and the confidence to do so.

BUT. The Indian Army counterparts were hellbent on stopping them in their tracks. A bit of a clash of interests resulting in a furious battle with the much publicised and reputed Patton tanks.

Bhoop recalls:

"I was asked to lead a four aircraft formation to provide close support to army in that sector. With me were Flight Lieutenants Ahuja, SK Sharma, and Parulkar as Nos. 2, 3 and 4 respectively. We reached the battle zone at low level. It was an open ground with fields tilled and some crops standing, but the scenario was vastly different from what we saw the previous evening. It was full of activity and dust could be seen from miles. The rushing Patton tanks with their big tracks were churning huge columns of dust heading East through the open fields. It was easy to spot them as they appeared at the head of each dust streak."

"Target 3 O'clock. Switches On."

"3 Contact," Flight Lieutenant Sharma the sub-section leader confirmed.

"Pulling up for a left hand attack."

"Spread out to right," I called as I eased the aircraft nose up to gain height.

As I gained height I could see more of area, and lot many more tanks.

"Boy, what a spread. Take your pick and get as many as possible," I had thought.

I rolled into a shallow dive aiming at the lead formation of tanks from a height of about 1500 feet. The bottom diamond of my gyro gunsight resting at the middle of tank tracks.

"Steady, Steady, Yes, hold it," I found telling myself as I neared the target.

My fingers were itching to press the trigger; speed was 460 knots and still it was taking so long. At last, the tanks were in the firing range. I pressed the trigger:

"Swish-Swish," and the rockets streaked out from both sides of my aircraft leaving a thin white smoke trail and rapidly converged into the target.

I pulled out of the dive, tuned back and saw the tanks emitting smoke and small tongues of orange flame starting to appear.

After establishing visual contact with the rest of my

formation, I rolled in for one more attack and had two more tanks knocked out of commission.

Total tally for the formation was 9 tanks destroyed.

Not bad for a single mission.

We were still left with our gun ammunition which had not been used. Besides the tanks the ground was littered with a large number of Infantry vehicles and supply lorries supporting the armour thrust.

We expended the ammunition, setting ablaze and crippling a very large number of supply vehicles.

It was an extremely rich haul and, I feel, that this contributed in no small measure towards the final outcome of the battle where the Indian Army defeated the mighty Pakistani tanks, considered to be an invincible weapon of war till then.

It was one of the biggest tank battles which took place after the Second World War, and I feel proud to have been a part of it. The area earned the name of, 'Grave Yard of Pattons', or 'Patton Nagar'.

This battle had sealed the fate of the Pakistani ambitions of having an uninterrupted drive through to Delhi, and have a tea-party on the ramparts of Red Fort. This was the battle which, perhaps, marked the turning point of the 1965 Indo-Pak War where, a confident, or rather a over-confident Pakistan Army with its own vision of grandeur and invincibility, was brought down to earth. They had failed to appreciate that it takes two to play the game called 'War'.

22

THE FIGHTING FIVE RAID PESHAWAR

As Boss Verma (Squadron Leader JC Verma) with six Canberra bomber aircraft reached the RV (rendezvous) for the final run in before the PUP (Pull Up Point) for the daring attack on Peshawar airfield, he heard Bob Gautam loud and clear in his earphones.

"Boss this is Bob, there is heavy anti-aircraft flak upto and well above 5000 feet, suggest you step your height accordingly for the attack."

"Thanks Bob, Wilco" Boss Verma had replied coolly.

Boss Verma is a Rimcolian, just about an inch past five feet and no more. He was the popular, unflappable flight commander of the 'Tuskers' Squadron flying Canberras during the 1965 War.

The Tuskers have an elephant with a twisted tail as their emblem in the Squadron crest and their motto is '*Shakti Vijayetae*' (Strength is Victory).

Challenged

The Tuskers had been challenged, and they decided to

show off their might on September 14, 1965, by selecting Peshawar for a six aircraft raid. You see reaching Peshawar meant that Boss Verma had to fly his formation literally through the well defended heart of Pakistan right up to the end of the northern tip. It also meant, flying the Canberras to the extremes of their flying range, thereby reducing the tactical routing to the bare minimum because there is hardly any fuel to play around with. The biggest imponderable, were the recently acquired Paki star fighters (F-104) aircraft, with night interception capability and their much publicised air-to-air side-winder missile.

Boss had a variety of targets to attack with nearly 48000 lb of bomb load that his formation was carrying. They had the BPI (Bulk Petrol Installation), the hangers, runway, aircraft and the PAF Air Headquarters to hit.

□

He had carefully selected the route to keep the Paki radar confused and guessing all the time.

He had succeeded so far but Bob's message at the RV showed that the Pakis were ready and waiting to give his formation a warm welcome.

On the final run in, Boss Verma's tired eyes picked up the river bend shinning in all its glory in the moonlight towards the north, and north-east of Peshawar. Boss made the final correction at the PUP, pulled up steeply to his bombing height simultaneously looking for his target which was followed by five Canberras who had their respective targets to deal with. Bob Gautam as the pathfinder had done a wonderful job, not only by advising Boss and his formation to step up their height but by also dropping the TI (Target Indicator) bomb right in the beginning of the runway as planned.

Immediately after pulling up, Boss saw the Peshawar airfield, and simultaneously the anti-aircraft flak, the heaviest that he had seen since the beginning of the war. He inched up above the flak bursts. He didn't want to climb too high. His biggest worry was the F-104s, against which he had no defence except his wits. Boss knew that he was right in the Tigers' den and it was waiting and ready to pounce. But that precisely was the idea. To call the bluff.

Target

Boss lined up for his target the BPI.

"Steady, slight port, steady steady, steady," was his navigator giving the instructions from the bomb aimer's position.

"Bomb doors open", Alu transmitted.

Boss opened the bomb doors with the flick of the switch and eased throttles to maintain the bombing speed.

At last, what felt like eternity, Boss heard, what he wanted to hear most.

"Bombs gone."

The whole aircraft shook, as if in joy, as 8000 lbs of bombs left its belly heading down towards the BPI.

He turned hard port and headed north for the hills away from the flak and the radar eyes, before he could descend down to tree-top level again to head back home.

The five Canberras, similarly, found their targets, right and proper and despatched their bombs precisely where they were meant to go.

"Hey, Boss you left the BPI in a mess, it is bursting in flames."

"Nice Hit," it was Bob transmitting as Boss was going

with full throttles open for the hills.

He knew that, it wasn't home yet.

"I have a bandit on my tail" Goody, who is now an Air India pilot flying jumbo Jets, transmitted.

"Get down and head for the hills. Shake him off," Boss had called back.

"Boss, I think I have been hit but mercifully still flying," Goody called back the next moment.

Boss and the rest of the formation saw a big ball of fire, a kind of glow that lits up the whole sky.

"Poor Goody," thought Boss.

Goody still had his Lady Luck smiling at him.

The Star Fighter had fired the missile and missed!

The raid on Peshawar was a measure of the favourable air situation that we had achieved during the war. The Peshawar raid was planned more as a show of daring to hit the well defended Paki safe bastion and the Pakistan Air Force Air Headquarters, a kind of prestigious target. The results were far beyond expectations.

The BPI (Bulk Petrol Installation) at Peshawar had kept burning for days like the fire we had started at Karachi during the 1971 operations. Though not claimed by the 'Tuskers' because our claims require authentic verification, it is believed that one of the chance hits had got a sizeable number of PAF aircrews in their aircrew rest rooms. The PAF Air Headquarters, which is just next to the airfield along the Cantt. road was also hit.

23

KAPS YOU GOT HIM

Air Vice Marshal V Kapila Reminisces

"September 19, 1965 had dawned with its normal excitement and element of apprehension as to how the ground and air battles would go this day. The night had been restful—no disturbing air raid warnings, none since the PAF bomber was shot down a few nights ago on our airbase.

We had just finished lunch when a call came to provide four aircraft Escort Mission to a Mystere Strike Force which was to attack the enemy armour and other targets near Chhawinda (a village and a railway station near Sialkot).This was the day of a major tank battle at Chhawinda, and many air missions had been sent in earlier in the day.

Squadron Leader Denzil Keelor (later Air Marshal) was to lead this Escort Mission with Flight Lieutenant Munna Rai at No. 2. I, then a Flight Lieutenant, was to fly No. 3, the Deputy Leader, with Maya Dev as my Wing Man in No. 4 position. It was a rushed affair as there was not much time to the TOT (Time On Target).

The careful and meticulous planning stage and briefing were quickly gone over, and we started up to take off in our

Tiny Gnats, just after the Mystere Formation being led by JP. The take off and transit to target area were normal, all flown below the Pakistan Radar Horizon, skimming the countryside. Close to target area JP gave a 'Call' for the Strike Formation to check all armament and switches. At this stage, Maya had suddenly called out:

"2 Bogeys Left 11 O clock High."

Sure enough, the Bogeys were spotted by all. I spotted another two and called out the same to Denzil, the Leader. Thus, we saw four Sabres hovering over the area.

In the meantime, the Mystere Strike Leader had turned on to his target for the attack. The Sabres overhead had spotted the Mysteres Formation, and started diving towards them. A situation now arose where the Mysteres were about to be threatened by the Sabres.

We, flying the Gnats, had kept our cool, and delayed our turning, in a bid to avoid being spotted by the enemy Sabres. Thus we planned to achieve the 'Classic Sandwich' (the Sabres neatly brought in a trap with a bait ahead of them, and we sitting behind to shoot at them).

The Sabres oblivious of our tactical move, had pressed on to the Mysteres who were advised by us to head for home after delivering their armament stores at the enemy.

Denzil now threw a turn towards the Sabres Formation, and I delayed mine a little more. Consequently, we had the Sabres neatly trapped. Denzil was sneaking onto 2 aircraft at an angle of approximate 40 degree, and I was manoeuvring to the 6 O'Clock position of the other two aircraft.

It was a copybook exercise to be true, because sure enough, our Lead Pair was spotted by the Sabres who, therefore, promptly called off the attack on the Mysteres, and thereafter fought for their survival.

We were now down to about 100 feet or so when the Sabres turned in madly towards our formation. This was the beginning of their end. What ensued was a maze of R/T calls in perfect union and coordination between Denzil, myself and Maya Dev.

Munna had got separated after the first hard turn had been carried out. He had been told to head for home so as to avoid being caught alone in the enemy territory.

Hard Turns, Reversals, Yo Yos, Max throttle, Minimum manoeuvring speeds, use of stick, ailerons, rudder were gone through with precision, a result of our consistently high state and standard of training in Wolf Pack Squadron.

Aircraft were ahead at one moment and 90 degree off at another, skimming the tree-tops at all the time. Our combat was being fought between 150 to 500 feet. I finally jockeyed myself behind a Sabre at a range of about 150 to 200 yards. I got him fixed in my sights and opened up a short 1/4 second bursts. I had fired three short bursts when I realized I was closing-in too fast and needed to do something about it.

So, I eased off the hard left turn and pulled up with maximum power to reposition for another attack. I could smell the cordite and my sinews were turned in for a 'kill'. I felt that I had possibly missed the Sabre narrowly, when I got the fantastic call from Denzil:

"Kaps you have got him."

"Kaps he is going down."

"Kaps he has hit the ground."

This prompted me to relax the manoeuvre, reverse back and look below. That was the time I saw the big flash. It was instant when the Sabre had finally hit the ground and disintegrated, blowing up in a huge ball of fire.

Denzil told me that he was in contact with me, and reported his position. I saw him with a Sabre on the opposite side of the circle of turn. Denzil manoeuvred sharply, and went in to shoot down the second Sabre in our area. He closed in very rapidly and called out:

"I am firing at him."

I kept clearing his tail just as he had cleared mine.

Soon he broke off the attack as his guns had jammed!

The Sabre by now was down to about 100 feet trailing a plume of black smoke but still flying away west into sun, which by now was low in the horizon. As I had the Sabre in sight, I quickly accelerated and latched on behind him.

The Gnat's superior power to weight ratio and acceleration were my main advantages. As I tried to reduce the distance from about 3 kms to shooting kill range of approximately 400 to 500 yards, I soon had him in my gun sight with the Pipper on the cockpit, and the range markers clawing on the wing tips to indicate when the proper firing range had been reached.

Denzil was keeping my tail clear. As soon as I reached 500 yards, I steadied my aim and pressed the trigger.

There was no response!

I did a quick double check of all the switches and circuit breakers. All systems were GO.

I again tried to fire at the fast closing Sabre.

Again a painfully compelling silence.

I waited in vain for the Rat-a-tat of the guns and the smoother vibration below my feet to indicate the bullets leaving the guns, but to no avail.

We were low on fuel, deep inside Pakistan, and travelling

west deeper every second. So, we quickly called off the attack from the smoking Sabre and headed back towards our home base—Denzil and myself in Broad Front Formation for a while.

A quick R/T check was called by Denzil; no return call was received from Maya. He was not in sight. We got into a quick dialogue on R/T and tried to locate Maya.

Denzil and I separated from each other as we crossed over into our territory. We called up all the neighbouring bases and asked to keep a listening out watch for Maya.

Denzil landed back at home base. I had to divert to a neighbouring base due to unavoidable reasons. We both filed in our reports including all what transpired.

We had got our 'Kills'.

One Confirmed, one probable.

Our Cine cameras showed the results.

Seeing the results, we affirm that the camera never lies.

It confirmed our claims.

That is IT.

LUCK

Take a second look at what appears to be someone's good luck. You will find not good luck but preparation, planning and success producing thinking preceded by his good fortune. Take a second look at someone's bad luck and you will discover some specific reasons. What appears to be good luck is good judgement. A lot of bad luck is just bad judgment.

Anonymous

01 Aug 64: Air Marshal AM Engineer handing over to Air Marshal Arjan Singh (Air Chief Marshal, 15 Jan 65, and now Marshal). Also seen in the picture are AVM, Rajaram, Chaturvedi and Chatterjee (Later Air Marshals)

24

MAZI SHOOTS DOWN F-86

It was the tenth day of the War with Pakistan in 1965. We had foiled the Pakistani bid in Chhamb area to literally twist the 'Chicken's Neck'. The Pakistani boast to drive down the GT Road as conquering heroes, had been convincingly demolished by our sporting response and, as if to pay back the compliment, our boys had gone right up to the Shalimar Gardens on the outskirts of Lahore, and had their little picnic.

Why didn't we enter Lahore? That is another story for another time and place.

What I am going to tell you is about Mazi, my batchmate in Flying Academy. He got a *Vir Chakra* for shooting down a PAF (Pakistan Air Force) F-86 (Sabre) in an exciting dog fight near Lahore.

Mazi is five feet and, perhaps, no more, and that makes him ideal for any cramped fighter cockpit. He fits in rather well there and with room to spare. In a transport aircraft he will need a series of cushions to reach up to the controls. Frankly, his height is like a woman's age—a top secret. Even the Docs don't share it with you for fear of inviting Mazi's wrath for breach of promise, and good faith. You see, when

Mazi gets angry, he is very very angry with the typical Calcutta temper on a warm and humid day. He is slightly, just slightly balding without a trace of grey hair.

"Mazi, do you dye your hair?," I asked. "No," was his reply.

I believe him because in the East, the people seem to age slower and grey later. Don't ask me "Why?" May be it has something to do with weather, food habits, heredity or may be, it is God's gift. Look at a Naga or a Mizo. They look ageless.

Always young.

Back to the battle.

Nothing Succeeds Like Success

In the air battles we were having a very enthusiastic and a lively response from all our Squadrons, and our Fighter Boys were itching to get into live air combats and put their years of hard training to good use. We had already drawn the first blood, and had kept adding to our tally.

We had learnt our lessons fast. It always happens when you are faced with stiff challenges, and war is a high stake game with no compromises or holds barred. We had spotted the vulnerable holes in the defensive and offensive capability of the highly publicised and rated F-86s and the F-104s of PAF.

You know it is something like in Cricket. Imagine Imran Khan pounding down the field to hurl the ball at Sunil Gavaskar, and he promptly despatches it to the boundary. It makes the pacer furious, and in his anger he makes more mistakes. So was the case, perhaps, with PAF. They had better machines and weaponary, but somehow couldn't get their sums right. Of course, in air-to-air battles, nothing succeeds like success, and we certainly had the Lady Luck smiling back at us.

"How do you rate the PAF pilots?", I ask Mazi.

"Of course, they are good; damn good; a worthy opponent in a dog fight. Makes it that much more interesting," Mazi muses.

"Then how do you account for our success?"

"Simple. We are better," shoots back Mazi.

Laconic and convincing. Let us get on with Mazi's story.

It was around 3:30 pm when nothing seemed to be happening when suddenly the much awaited call had come; "Mission-33 Stand by Two."

This call brings the pilot to cockpit readiness, and the Fighter Pilot(s) sit in the cockpit of their aircraft and wait for further instructions.

Mazi and Kamli Khanna, his No. 2, had run out to their Tiny Gnats at the ORP (Operational Readiness Platform). The next call wasn't long in coming.

"Mission-33 Scramble", and the controller had given the initial Vector and the height to climb to. Two Gnats and two Hunters had got airborne and were heading for where the real action was.

"Will we get them," was the main thought on Mazi's and Kamli Khanna's mind.

The Pakistanis had a distinct advantage on two counts: firstly, they certainly had a better radar coverage which as you know is the eyes of the modern high performance aircraft. Secondly, they were on their own home ground.

Mazi and his formation was heading west towards Lahore with, unfortunately, little help from our own radar. Instinct plays a vital role in the game called fighter flying; your gut feeling somehow tells you the right things, and Mazi could smell trouble, or shall we say action, that lay only a few moments ahead. He could see Lahore coming up under his nose while flying at 15000 feet.

They have got to be around, Mazi had reasoned to himself.

He had ordered a hard Port (Left) turn, and it was during this turn that he had spotted what he was looking for, and this was just about in time.

What he saw was four Sabres in line astern position on his tail at about 2000 yards, fast closing-in for the 'kill'. Obviously, the Pakistanis had the radar cover, and their fighter controller had done a damn good job in positioning his fighters behind our for a simple kill. It was a lucky break for Mazi, and once again, he had that gut feeling that it was his day. He had just averted a major problem by sighting the PAF aircraft just in the nick of time.

"Not yet son; you have not got me till you get me," Mazi got his act together to salvage a potentially dangerous situation. He still had to turn the tables on the PAF fighters who had a distinct advantage in having been positioned right behind our fighters. But, Mazi still had a trick or two up his sleeve.

Soon it was a free for all; eight Jets weaving patterns in the sky and trying to get on the other's tail for the kill. This ballet-in-the-sky had carried on for what seemed to be an interminably long time—almost for four odd minutes—the kind of time Mazi could ill afford to spend over the enemy territory.

Then Mazi had got the break he had been looking for. He spotted a F-86 neatly lined-up behind our Hunter aircraft which was fast closing in for the kill. Mazi had opened throttle and with better acceleration, had pounced on F-86, and had closed-in not quite at the recommended speed, you rarely do so in actual combat.

"I gave the first quarter burst at about 200 yards," recalls Mazi, "followed by another burst."

"Then what happened?"

Mazi can never forget the sight.

"After the first burst, the pilot had made up his mind to eject and his canopy flew off as he pulled his ejection seat handle, and the next moment his aircraft was a ball of fire. The whole sequence is on my cine film."

"What happened to pilot?"

"I saw him sailing down with his parachute. He must have been picked up immediately because we were quite close to Lahore."

Then? There seemed to be peace.

"Kamli's trigger finger was itching but there was nothing to shoot at. We did not want to stretch our luck with the fuel running low."

Mazi looked up at me.

"Why do you want to write this old story?," he asks. "Because I hadn't heard it before. Had you?"

Remnants of a Pak Sabre shot down at Halwara

25

APPEASEMENT AND COMPLACENCY: SOME LEAVES FROM HISTORY

Complacency and appeasement are an absolute NO NO in all aspects of life and spell disaster when practiced in politics and more so in the defence forces. The War Histories are full of instances when this twin affliction of appeasement and complacency cost the nations dearly. Duplicity and double-speak are a part of diplomacy as well as military strategy. There is nothing new about it.

Sun Tzu, the Military Analyst and Strategist—served as a Staff Officer and General to King Ho Lu, the King of Wu. He is supposed to have impressed the king with his mastery of drills, manoeuvres, discipline and the authority of Field Commander and Commander-in-Chief. The oft quoted example is the drilling by Sun Tzu of 180 beautiful concubines of the king. Sun Tzu, undoubtedly, understood the importance of clear orders and implicit obedience, so vital to the battle worthiness of a professional army.

Sun Tzu wrote his most fascinating book, *The Art of War*, around 4500 BC. He, like Confucius was a great thinker. The

Art of War is thoughtful, comprehensive and an imaginative treatise on the military principles. Even today in the world of Conventional Wars and Nuclear environment, this book has a reputation without parallel. Says Sun Tzu:

"All warfare is based on deception. A skilled General must be a master of the complementary arts of simulation and dissimulation; while creating shapes to confuse and delude the enemy, he conceals his true dispositions and ultimate intent. When capable, he feigns incapacity; when near, he makes it appear that he is far away; when far away he makes it appear that he is near. Moving as intangibly as a ghost in star-light, he is obscure and inaudible. His primary target is the mind of the opposing Commander. The victorious situation is the product of imagination. An indispensable preliminary to battle is to attack the mind of the enemy."

Says Chang Yu, another Chinese military thinker: "When enemy's envoy speaks in humble terms, but continues his preparations He will advance." In the same vein, says Ch'en Hao: "When without previous understanding the enemy asks for truce; he is plotting." And an ageold proverb says: "It is double pleasure to deceive a deceiver."

It is a fighter pilot's dictum that there is nothing great to die for one's country. Victories are won by making the other guy die for his country.

These are the facts of real life where idealism has a very limited space to jostle for. Let us have a look at a few wrong turns of history which extracted a heavy cost in terms of men, money and machines.

Hitler's Bluffs

When Hitler occupied Rhineland, everyone of his Generals and most of his advisors had cautioned him against it, saying that it would invite instant retaliation. In the event, not a single shot was fired!!

Hitler became invincible.

Hitler's road to domination was opened.

In 1936, Hitler could have been expelled from Rhineland and thus booted out of power with a loss of no more than a dozen lives. Because he was allowed to get away with his fortifications in Rhineland, it eventually took 50 million dead to rid the world of one mad man.

When Hitler had followed up his occupation of Rhineland by annexing Austria, Churchill had used his now historically famous rebuke of the government:

"You are adamant only to be undecided;
Resolved to be irresolute;
Adamant for drift;
Solid for fluidity;
All powerful to be impotent."

Hitler had affirmed that there was no such thing as Austria: Austria was Germany. When Hitler for a while had desisted from capturing Czechoslovakia, Chamberlain went to Munich to return with a piece of paper proclaiming:

"I have got it. I believe it is peace for our time."

Hitler's lunge to capture the Danzing Corridor in Poland was apparently what brought World War II. Most Westerners had thought that Hitler had a pretty good claim on Danzing. Yet 50 million people died because by the time of Hitler's invasion of Poland, even Chamberlain could take it no more.

Hitler got away with swallowing Czechoslovakia, notwith-standing Munich and all the gibberish about, "Peace for our time." Chamberlain's objective should never have been appeasement of Hitler. There can be no appeasement of those who are determined to wage war—whatever the cost.

NO TRAP IS SO DEADLY—AS THE ONE YOU SET FOR YOURSELF.

Nearer Home

One could go on writing about the instances of complacency, appeasement and overconfidence which cost the nations very dearly. Let us have a close look at a few instances nearer home.

The intent and content of Appeasement and Complacency must be understood in the right context. The spirit of give-n-take to cut down on losses and get the value for money is not appeasement. Appeasement is turning a blind eye to the bluffs and bluster of the other party, as we saw the British doing in Thirties towards the acts and aggressive postures of Hitler.

Similarly, complacency implies to let down your guard and expose yourself in the belief that, as Chamberlain said, "You have got peace during your times." Not to be complacent implies the dictum, "Never trust anyone even if you pretend to."

Let me take you down the memory lane of history and tell you a short story from the pages of our history. Ahmed Shah Abdali was one of the most ruthless and greedy conquerors who had made it a habit to roll down the Indian plains with his hordes and go back with all the riches he wanted and more. People were not only fed up but mortally scared of him because nothing was sacred to him.

The Marathas had taken on the task to tame the invader and moved up north to stop Ahmed Shah Abdali in his tracks and teach him a lesson so that he did not dare to come down to India on his Loot-Runs. They were well prepared for it and had mustered a numerical superiority of 1:10 that will deter any invader. What is more they were good fighters and had a reputation to fight to the last man. The Battle Lines had been drawn.

Ahmed Shah Abdali came down and did stop in his tracks. He was a good fighter and a General. He certainly did not want to embroil his outnumbered troops in a losing fight. But soon he got thinking as to why the Marathas were not on the offensive. His operatives came back with the news that the Marathas as advised by their *Jyotshi* (Astrologer) were waiting for the right time to strike when the stars are right.

Abdali had promptly laid a siege at Panipat, and soon enough the Maratha Army was reduced to eating their own horses and famished.

Ahmed Shah Abdali had no qualms about the position of stars and so on. He relied more on his commonsense and opportunities, which he was good at creating.

When Ahmed Shah Abdali, quite unaided by his Astrologers which, in any case he had none, struck, it took him just under three hours to rout the Marathas, and had his fill of the riches of India undeterred.

In October 1947 Kashmir Operations, we should have been smart enough to realize that the British interests did not quite tally with our national interests. It was quite evident right from the word go, and with a little more pluck and courage by our politicians we should have been able to clear the J&K of all the raiders. That was not to be, and for that political insensitivity or call it, incorrect readings we have paid and are yet paying a very heavy price.

Prior to 1962, once again we had displayed appeasement and undue idealistic trust in the Chinese intentions. The Chinese subtleties were alien to us. We forced ourselves into a unequal battle because we didn't know what we want, nor how to get it. 'Throwing the Chinese Out', and 'Not surrendering an inch of Indian territory to the Chinese', was a tall order considering our military preparedness and the envisaged task. It was a political disaster and military humiliation, both of which could and should have been avoided with a little more care and political shrewdness.

In April 1965, after the Kutch episode we had assumed that we had bought peace. We saw the ominous clouds on the horizon, but carried out half-hearted preparations only. We were surprised, or shall we say, unprepared to meet the Pakistani onslaught on September 1, 1965, when it appeared that General Ayub Khan was all set to have his tea party on the ramparts of Red Fort in Delhi. Thanks to the prompt response by the IAF the Pakistani Armour onslaught at Chhamb was stopped in its tracks giving the Army some breathing time to get its sums right.

Operation Cactus Lily, 1971 War, was a planned war where right from the word go, we held the aces and went about the operation in a clinical and a efficient way with speed and purpose, because our aims were well-defined and there was no ambiguity.

Sri Lankan Odyssey was a classical case of getting all our sums wrong and paying a very heavy price. We had failed to read the situation and put all our trust in the Sri Lankan Accord. We misread the LTTE; we got the Sri Lankan Government's aims all wrong, and we went into action as if it was a picnic.

Operation Vijay—the Kargil Fiasco is another classical case of appeasement and complacency. We refused to believe the obvious. We were totally drunk in the euphoria of the

Lahore Bus ride. We refused to use the historical references in the Indo-Pak relations where the handshakes and the *Japhees* last only as long as they do, and the moment you have disengaged, it is back to India baiting, as far as Pakistan is concerned.

I think we have a lot to learn from the Chinese in the art of diplomacy and war. They have a delightful trait of being able to walk-their-talk, and when they find that the road is rather rough for a walk, they do not talk. Similary, they are past masters in their appreciation of the Art-of-the-possible. They hate to waste their words or efforts. For them the grip and the duration of the handshake is a clear enough indication on the depth and mutuality between the nations. Their priorities are quite clear and well-defined, and that is what makes them a nation which cannot be taken lightly.

Time for us to introspect and try and figure out what our priorities should be—joining the race to Mars; landing at Moon; to be in the Also-rans; may be to take seriously our defence production, the defence forces; not forgetting the common man who is still starved of the basics like water, electricity, education, health care and so on.

What ARE our priorities?

What should they be?

Before we start we must know our destination because then alone you will be able to take the right road. Otherwise, you are likely to end up on a road which takes you nowhere, as has been happening in most of our ambitious projects.

Handing over the reins of IAF to Air Chief Marshal PC Lal

26

A BRIEF HISTORY OF OUR UNWRITTEN WAR HISTORIES

In his Foreword, for one of our earlier books, *Profiles Of Courage* Air Chief Marshal Arjan Singh had written:

"The Defence apparatus of the country has been a sacred cow; debates on various aspects of security have been discouraged in the Parliament and amongst public. This has, in a way, resulted in the inadequacy of planning and proper equipment, there has been much *ad hocism* and reaction to events rather than a long term plan. This is partly due to a lack of strategic intelligence and assessment of future threats.

The 1965 War with Pakistan had brought out our weaknesses in this respect. Despite intrusion by Pakistan into J&K by its Regulars and Mujahidins etc., we did not clearly foresee that Pakistan may attack in strength, we were unable to assess that the attack may be launched with a view to cutting off our links of communication to Poonch and to the Kashmir Valley. The attack on the Chhamb-Jaurian Sector on September 1, 1965, was a surprise and swift in execution. We were falling back to armour attack and Akhnur bridge was in danger."

□

Have we learnt all our lessons from the wars fought? Let us have a close hard look at the history of the unwritten war histories instead of treating them like a 'SACRED COW', as Air Chief Marshal put it.

A Saga of Dangerous Delusions

See no evil.

Hear no evil.

Speak no evil.

That's the Gandhian principle that has been diligently applied to the process of writing our war histories since independence. Our politicians and bureaucrats, not forgetting the men-in-uniform, seem to have discovered a magic *Mantra* in the words, "The information continues to be classified and cannot be divulged in public interest."

Full Stop

That's the end of the road. The dead end. Ask no questions and thou shall be told no lies. That's the *Mantra* that's handed down to every Defence Minister by the bureaucrats, and that conveniently puts an end to any possibility of a dialogue or a discussion, if the themes happen to be inconvenient, or a reflection on the inefficiency of the people-who-matter.

It is a dangerous delusion that the issues or the truths will melt away with the all-too-frequent stone-walling even on minor questions, not forgetting the most-talked-about and common knowledge happenings in the conduct of war, and the deficiencies in the command and control responsibilities and accountability. The end result is that, in the consequent

witch-hunt, we find a bewildered scapegoat down-the-line, which does not know what hit it, and is in no position to counter the 'Guilty' verdict. The scapegoat is sacrificed with all the pomp and righteousness, and no tears are shed.

SOON. Sooner than expected, it is business-as-usual.

Get the Facts Right

The aim of writing history is not only to place the facts on record for the future generations, but it also helps in improving our tactics in the future strategic planning. In the absence of an honest appraisal, how can the army learn from its mistakes, without knowing what they were? It is about time that we appreciate the relevance of the old adage, 'Those who do not learn from the past mistakes, are condemned to repeat them'.

And admittedly, we have been doing precisely that—from one conflict to the other, from one war to the other. And, worse still, no one seems to care, not even the Armed Forces at the right level who are in a position to influence the course of events. It has almost become a case of, 'No one wants to bell the cat', that is till the cat is in the chair, and after that, the common brotherhood of 'You scratch my back and I'll scratch yours' takes over.

And the important lessons of war are given a decent burial, till their rebirth in the next conflict, in a more aggravated form, and expected disasters and losses which in the first place could have been avoided if we had taken care to learn from our mistakes. And thus the cycle goes on, uninterrupted, and with no signs of possible change, just because the present system suits the chairborne warriors.

We seem to have mastered the art of concealing the unpleasant truths and facts under the obsolete omnibus

Official Secrets Act which was spelt out by the British primarily to keep the natives on the minimum information level. That suited the British. After all the natives were not involved in any sort of planning exercises. But back home, it is a different ball game and the truth, no matter how unpleasant, is rarely managed to be kept under the wraps.

Undoubtedly, not recording the political history or doctoring it, will have some effect, but as far as the military history is concerned, suppressing the facts and truth have a very damaging effect and hurts the nation a lot more than it would have if the truth is placed on record.

Writing the military history is not a new trend. In fact, our actions before independence have been far better recorded than our present recordings since independence, that is, whatever little has been recorded and made available for the general public. Writing war histories is not something new where we are trying to set a global precedent, or something that might compromise our national interests or security. In fact, it is a very very important add-on for the defence planning. It is a MUST, if our planning has to be realistic and effective. Histories have been written by all major countries, and continue to be written for all the conflicts. Former British Prime Minister, Sir Winston Churchill wrote four volumes on World War II as did General Eisenhower (later President of USA) and Marshal Zhukhov (Soviet Defence Minister).

Whatever few books have been written in India on the defence themes are mostly authored by retired defence officers and that too after they have exhausted the post retirement perks that the government can offer, and they feel safe enough, or are beyond caring, that they sit down to pen their thoughts(?), many many years later, when the memory has faded, and they have no access to the official records to verify the facts. The aim is, obviously, self-promotion, justifications, or an ego-trip, not forgetting, may be to settle old scores, and personal opinions which have little value at such a late stage, because the times are changing fast. Nevertheless, they do help to fill the odd gaps in history, and in some cases, the plain speaking has exploded many myths, perhaps, the main reason(s) why the official history has neither been recorded or published.

They do serve a purpose, and let me say, "Keep punching out your stories, and don't hesitate to dip your pen in acid." For, you never know, it might, just might, erode the official rust gathered on the deep truths buried below. Also, it might, just might, provoke the smug bureaucracy to react and respond more positively instead of facing the truths at a later stage. Patriotism and national spirit demand that.

Some Examples

If our war histories had been honestly recorded, it should have forewarned us, and made us ask the right kind of questions, and prepare for the future in a more logical manner both militarily and politically. Let us have a close-hard look at a few glaring examples.

Operation Gulmarg: Kashmir Operations according to unofficial published sources, there is a reason to believe that the British were in total picture about the Pakistani plans to grab Kashmir, and if anything, they had gone out of their way to make it a success. The Pakistani plan was formulated immediately after Independence in August, 1947. Yet, we were told only when the raiders were on the outskirts of the Srinagar airfield, though, according to the Pakistani planners they should have been in Srinagar town by that time. Delay was caused by the unscheduled orgy of rape, loot, murder and barbarism by the raiders in Baramula, which could be stopped only with the promise that there was more of it to be had at Srinagar, and the so-called liberators fighting a holy war, had moved on with the sure knowledge that there was nothing to stop them from restarting their session of orgy at Srinagar by the end of the day.

This aspect should have been taken seriously the moment we got to know of it, and should have formed an important part of our recorded history. Not only that, our blind trust in the British sincerity should have been revised. Had we done that, we wouldn't have gone to UN when we did, and when the total victory was just a whisper away.

The only official record of the 1962 Sino-India conflict so far is the Inquiry Report on The Indian Debacle by the late Lieutenant General Thomas Bryan Henderson Brookes, an Anglo-Indian Army officer. Till today, the Henderson Brookes Report remains classified though portions of it, it is alleged, have been leaked to a foreign author to help him write a book which is not flattering to the Indian government.

Interestingly, according to published sources, the Henderson Brookes Committee never had access to Top Secret Documents from the Directorate of Military Operations. Another aspect of this report is that while Henderson Brookes was only a Corps Commander, he was entrusted and expected to comment on the tactical decisions and actions by several officers much senior to him. It is also an open secret that the Report was mainly authored by Lt Gen PS Bhagat, who was Director of Military Intelligence (DMI) till mid-1962, which was only months before the

Chinese troops crossed the Indian borders, and logically he should have known about the Chinese build-up as the DMI, and should have been the one answering a lot of questions, and not writing a report on the debacle. Surprisingly, even then the report has not been made public till date.

What really happened at Sela Pass? Was it a case of Chinese human waves and the overwhelming superiority in men and machines which made our troops abandon their well dug in and fortified positions and run? According to the unofficial first person accounts of the officers who were at Sela Pass, there was not a single shot fired by us or the Chinese, nor were there any Chinese troops threateningly close when we ran, leave aside the human waves! What is the truth? More so, because many officers have been decorated for their bravery(?) in the face of the enemy.

According to another published report, a team of military officers under the eminent historian, Nandan Prasad, did compile a detailed report on the 1965 and 1971 Indo-Pak Wars, but it was scrutinized by a committee of Secretaries who had little knowledge of the wars, and went on a editing spree to conform to the various views, as result of which serious distortions had crept in. It is believed that 100 copies of an abridged version of the edited 1971 War report have been published. The restricted circulation of the report is not known.

It is an open secret in Army that, in 1965, General JN Choudhuri had asked Army Commander, Western Command, Lt Gen Harbaksh Singh, to withdraw his forces to Beas river, when Pakistan had launched a massive armoured thrust in Punjab's Khem Karan Sector. Had this been done, and had we allowed the Pakistanis to reach Beas river with their armour, the end story would certainly have been a lot different, disastrous and humiliating. Full marks to the Army Commander for giving the Pakistani armour a bloody nose in the Khem Karan Sector at Assal Uttar, and converting it into a graveyard of Patton tanks, instead of retreating to Beas river.

On the negative side, Lt Gen Harbaksh Singh, according to the published sources, was, perhaps, responsible for the humiliating surrender of the Sikh Regiment, of which he was the Colonel Commandant. This had given Pakistanis a publicity handle which they had exploited to the hilt. The task given to the regiment to capture Khem Karan was mindless, and well beyond their potential, and the Army Commander should have known this. In all fairness, this aspect should have been looked into with impartiality and his name cleared of the allegations, or held him responsible for the error of his judgment.

There are any number of Ifs and Buts of the 1965 and 1971 Wars which should have been seriously and diligently analysed, not with a view to let down anyone or to find a scapegoat, but to draw the relevant lessons. Every engagement reflects the enemy's mindset and his line of thinking, and as has been wisely said, to win a war you have first to try and figure out what the enemy commander thinks. Of course, war is a very unforgiving game, and the price one has to pay for miscalculations or incompetence can be immense, and as such you HAVE to make sure that you have the right guys at the top posts.

If we had learnt our lessons in 1965, there was no reason for us to repeat our mistakes in Chhamb Sector and elsewhere, precisely as we had done in 1965, and ended up losing territory. Knowing Rajasthan Sector to be a vast area and a favourite with the Pakistani planners for land grab, yet we had Longewala incident which nearly presented our Jaisalmer airbase and other vital areas on a platter to Pakistan, but for the pluck-n-courage of a handful of Hunter pilots of Triple Two Squadron, who managed to turn the Pakistani near perfect plan inside out. We didn't have a clue till they were there knocking on our front door.

We had tried to rationalise our performance in the western sector in 1971 with a cute little explanation that, in the west we were fighting a defensive battle. But what is a defensive battle? You defend only when you cannot attack. We didn't have a defensive plan like the Hitler's Atlantic Wall, or the French Maginot Line which Hitler had overrun earlier in the initial stages of World War II, and triumphantly marched into Paris. We did not achieve the desired results in western sector in 1971 because we had failed to learn from our mistakes in 1965 and, worse still, have done precious little to overcome our shortcomings. Pakistan had no surprises, and had acted and reacted all along on the predictable lines throughout the war.

But nothing to beat the Kargil Fiasco. Despite the media going hammer and tongs for the bureaucrats and the higher echelons of Army Staff, and exposing our weaknesses in our command and control at higher levels, one would have hoped that this is one conflict which will make us learn our lessons, the right ones. But. What have we got?

We have got the Subramaniam Report which keeps everybody happy. There were no failures. What happened was beyond the human control because we didn't have the superhuman gadgetery with us. In short, it was inevitable under the circumstances.

We needed a scapegoat, and we found one in the shape of the Kargil Brigade Commander. He was the villain, and he was a very useful piece because all the mud you threw, you could make it stick on him. He did put up a fight, a sort of it, but then he was fighting a system, an organisation, which is always unbeatable, and is always right, no matter how wrong they are.

It has been conveniently forgotten that he had asked for the same moon which the Army is NOW asking for, and it is believed that it is what Subramaniam Committee has recommended. Forgotten also is the fact that Kargil and the areas around had literally become a Practice Firing Range for the Pakistani Gunners, and they had been carrying out some pinpoint blasting and blowing up our ammunition depots, TV Towers, and the rest with incredible accuracy and ease. And, yet, all the way up, it was passed off as routine. The Kargil Brigade Commander's reports were ignored as 'Alarmist', and as one who was trying to corner glory out of routine happenings. So the bosses thought all the way up. And yet, when the things went wrong, he is the guy who had the full blast of blame from all the corners.

Let us learn our first important lesson that when the things go wrong during a conflict, the Buck does not stop at the Platoon, Regiment, Battalion or a Brigade level unless it happens to be a case of cowardice or plain sabotage as we had witnessed in 1962. The Buck has to stop at the Army HQs, which is supposed to be a lot more than a mere Operations Room collecting and collating the SITREPS(Situation Reports). This is not to defend or accuse the Kargil Brigade Commander who is under Cloud Nine, but to say that the Responsibility and Accountability must be correctly assigned at the correct level.

Here is a classical case of taking responsibility, and I quote President Vladimir Putin on the loss of Russian Submarine KURSK killing all the 118 crew members, "I bear a feeling of full responsibility and a feeling of guilt for this tragedy. The Defence Minister and several Naval Chiefs have offered their resignations, but no one will be fired until a full investigation has been conducted. It would be an easy route for me to take, but I will not accept any resignations now. If anyone is to be blamed he will have to be punished. But first we must get a clear picture of the causes of this tragedy...."

Have we got the clear picture of what happened in 1947-1948; 1962,1965, 1971, and now the Kargil Fiasco?

Another relevant point that comes up is that, if we had assimilated our 1965 lessons, we would have realized and appreciated the folly of sacking the operational commanders in the midst of short duration conflicts, which do not offer you the luxury of the winning Generals to come up in the course of a long duration war like the World War II. The sackings and removals demoralise the troops and eats into fighting efficiency.

The selection of operational commanders is a serious business, and not a mere 'ticket punching' for the higher ranks. Once you have selected the Commander to lead the troops in war, he must be allowed to perform. During the Operation Vijay we had the spectre of the commanders being removed from the fighting zones on medical grounds!! And a casual look reveals that we had Battalion Commanders in the age of Fifties. Has the enhancement of two years service at the higher ranks got something to do with this? It is something that requires a serious thought, because fighting formations cannot possibly afford to take on the additional task of providing employment to the old and the frail.

Happily for us, Pakistan, our main if not the only adversary with whom we had a few war-games at regular intervals, has shown the same sense of urgency as ours, in recording their war histories. I am sure that their reason(s) for not recording must be the same compulsions as ours. The result has been that they have launched their successive offensives by pulling out the same old war plans. Happily for them, they found us responding the same old way, and so the show goes on.

General Pervez Musharraf did show some pluck in the Kargil Fiasco, and had us nicely cornered trying to figure out our answers. But, he had failed to take into account all the factors, and that is why it is apt to call it a Fiasco for both the sides. Being so recent, and so well covered it needs no recounting.

Lastly, in this scenario of no authentic war records, it will do us a lot good to examine and accept our victory in 1971 in the correct perspective, instead of over-rating our capabilities and performances. Worse than not recording the history, is to draw selective lessons, and give yourself a tag of invincibility. Today, war is a fast moving affair and it brooks no delays or complacency. Individual courage, unorthodox responses and tactics do play a very important role in any engagement, but cannot replace the need to be suitably armed, clothed and a sound logistics backup. Trying to go on a shopping spree for the arms and spares in the midst of a short duration conflict makes no sense.

Media Vs Establishment

Let us get a few facts right. It is not the job of the Media to write History. Media reports what they see, what they hear, perhaps, sensationalise a bit, and then give out a readable story. It is based on limited exposure, limited time frame, and a limited knowledge. What it gives is a lead to what is happening as they observe, and undoubtedly, form a very important input in recording the history at a later date.

It is the historian's job to record the facts, the TRUTH. He has the time and the resources to dig out the facts and then record them. He is not a man in a hurry like a Reporter who has a deadline to meet.

It is not the historian's job to grade the Commanders' performance, or to analyse the tactics or strategies unless the inputs are from qualified persons.

There has been a degree of intermixing of roles where the media has tried to take on the role of a historian and the historian attempting to write the Performance Appraisal of Commanders.

Mr SN Prasad, the general editor of the official history of 1965 Indo-Pak War, in an interview with Mr Manoj Joshi, in *Times of India* dated September 25, 2000, says:

General JN Choudhury, the Army Chief during the war, was, let us say, moderately competent—yet he went far. (Major General) Niranjan Prasad was a little better than him, but he had bad luck both in 1962 and in 1965. (Lt Gen) BM Kaul was exceptionally able in general matters, but turned out to be unlucky."

What the historian can and should do is to dig out the facts, and then state them. To give you an example, accusations were being made that in 1944, George Bush, the future 41st President of USA, a Torpedo Bomber Pilot, had attacked an unarmed trawler and not a Japanese warship as claimed by him. His name was cleared in 1994 when the wreckage of the Japanese ship was located. Sitting on what was left of the deck, were gun mounts and a big pile of ammunition.

That is what history is all about.

Let me give you another example of how the Media can hound the establishment and hunt for the truth. During my recent visit to USA in April-June 2000, there was an interesting (Ethical) battle raging between the media and the establishment regarding the alleged 'Turkey Shoot', by a US infantry Division under the Command of now (Retd) Four Star General McCaffery, against defeated Iraqi Columns who were going back home after the ceasefire.

Febled War Correspondent Seymour M Hersh, has alleged that a US Mechanised Division massacred retreating Iraqi troops in 1991 Gulf War, and has urged thorough investigation into the incident. He has carefully documented his charges which are based on 300 interviews conducted over six months. He has reconstructed one of the most one-sided victories in the US Military annals. According to Hersh:

"Two days after the Gulf ceasefire, 24th Infantry Division of US Army demolished a retreating Iraqi Republican Guards Tank division near Rumalia Oilfield at hardly any cost to American life."

Hersh's article alleges that Major General Barry McCaffery attacked without serious provocation in pursuit of glory.

This just about shows the important role of the Media to ensure that the sanitised version of the official histories do

not bury the deeper truths.

Let me end this 'Brief History of Our Unwritten War Histories', with what Mr Aroon Purie has to say on the subject in his Edit Page of *India Today* of August 12-15, 2000:

"There is no escaping history. Sometimes we celebrate the past but there are occasions when it comes back to haunt us. Either way there is no escape. This week's story is a remembrance of what was momentous year: 1971. The war that year created not only just history but, literally geography, a new country Bangladesh was born. For India, it signalled its most decisive military victory since Independence. In Pakistan it was perceived as a betrayal of the idea of a nation founded only on religion. As society it has not quite lived down 1971, and somewhere in the militarised psyche there is a thirst for Retribution, and the desire to explain the defeat in terms of complex conspiracy theories."

Shortly, after the surrender of Dacca in December, 1971, Pakistan's new ruler, Zulfiqar Ali Bhutto, set up a commission to inquire into the debacle. Headed by the then Chief Justice, the Commission concluded that Pakistan's defeat stemmed from the greed, perversions and mismanagement of its Army Generals. The report makes a fascinating reading. In fact, it was so damning in its indictment of the military elite that Bhutto immediately suppressed it and claimed to have burnt every copy. At least one survived and, through an elaborate network of sources and intermediaries, found its way after 26 years to *India Today* Group Online's General Manager (Content Services) Samar Halarnkar. He poured over it to write an article whose revelations are bound to add a valuable dimension to any assessment of contemporary history. It tells us how Pakistan analysed the war then, whatever it may say now. There is some irony that Pakistan is once again under the thumb of a military dictatorship, determined to take the country on the course it decides. Islamabad has not learnt from the past. Nor, indeed, has Delhi; The Henderson Brookes Report on the defeat to the Chinese in 1962 has still not been declassified.

So, what's the message here?
Don't try and hide from truth.
It has an uncanny habit of catching up.
Is anyone listening?

HISTORY

The practical value of history is to throw the film of past through the material projector of the present on to the screen of the future.

Liddel Hart

To write true history is always offensive to those who have an interest in concealing.

Graffiti

It might be a good idea if various countries of the world would occasionally swap history books just to see what other people are doing with the same set of facts.

Bill Vaughan

27

TURNS TAKEN AT THE CROSSROADS: SOME COMMON DENOMINATORS

All the conflicts we have fought so far since Independence had a few common denominators primarily because we seem to have missed the Turning Points after each conflict, and merrily continued to travel along the wrong roads leading to the same destination Up-The-Gum-Tree.

The first Turning Point is our inability to have been able to evolve a credible and a quick response institutional structure. In every conflict it has taken us painfully long to realize the enormity of the situation and then start looking for effective response. It has, invariably, taken us awfully long to get our act together when the war is upon us. It is all the more important for us to be able to respond quickly and effectively because of our policy of waiting for the aggressor to make the first move at a time and place of his choice. Any delays in our response put us at a great disadvantage and invariably we have ended up paying a heavy price in men and material, and taken much longer to develop our own offensive options.

The Second Turning Point that we seem to have missed is to evolve and have a credible and effective Integrated War-Fighting Machine. Our various Inter-Service Committees notwithstanding, there appears to be little effort to present a 'Joint Solution' to a potential threat. What we have been able to achieve so far is that when the war is already upon us, we get down to the task and try and work out an improvised Integrated response to the fast developing situations. The war, more so today, is an Integrated affair where the enemy is made to feel the full brunt of the three arms—Army, Navy and Air Force. Of course the Navy and the Air Force have their own primary commitments to keep the sea-lanes free from enemy interference, and for the Air Force to achieve a degree of air superiority soonest besides guarding their own airbases. Nevertheless, there is enough punch to spare to join some result-oriented fireworks and put the enemy on the defensive.

The Third Turning Point which, apparently, we have refused to take despite its staring in our face almost daily is the unchanged image of the Indian Jawan—ill-clothed and ill-equipped in peace as well as war. It is hard to believe that it is because of the cash-crunch. Perhaps, it is because of the insatiable greed of the concerned agencies. In the modern trend of wars which are swift and of short duration, you enter and finish the war on as-you-are basis. It is foolish to try and go on a shopping spree to make good the deficiencies when the guns are booming.

The Fourth Turning Point is the tendency to fight the war with war manual in hand, and the manuals we have are the World War I vintage. That won't do. The modern wars call for a lot of innovations and improvisations BUT the basic

requirement is that you must have the right tools.

The last but not the least is that each of our conflicts has been presented to us as a surprise, a BIG SURPRISE. Intelligence Failure has been the most shrill cry heard after each conflict.

It is time that we got on the right roads and then start inching towards the right destination, and not keep going downhill at break-neck speed, as we have been doing so far.

Pakistan started all the wars with India on the premise that India could not match the Pakistan's military prowess. Kargil amply showed our operational attitude of, 'not-to-trouble-trouble-till-the-trouble-troubles-you'. It showed our total lack of proactive and anticipatory assessment, and accordingly the ability to make timely preparations to counter it. Even when the local Commanders did try and put across the likely emerging scenarios they were shooed away as alarmist and glory-seekers without verifying or atleast accepting them as plausible and making preparations accordingly.

Our lackadaisical attitude towards national security is only a part of the overall culture of superficiality and indifference on all aspects of public issues including defence by the politicians who still seem to have that colonial hangover that the natives are the lesser beings and should be happy with whatever crumbs are thrown at them.

The reason for this is ONE LACK OF COMMITMENT TO THE NATION AND ITS GOVERNANCE. Governance means there is one 'governor' the Fountain Head who spells out the rules of the game. The problem arises when everybody becomes a governor and lays down his own rules—a set of rules for himself, and another one for others. It is time, infact overdue, that we took the right road and got our sums right for decision making structures and procedures which should be continuously monitored and maintained to ensure that they do not become dysfunctional and continue to operate efficiently.

Leading From the Front

If the world is to be brought to order
My nation first must be changed
If my nation is to be changed
My home-town must be made over
If my home-town is to be re-ordered
My family first must be set right
If my family is to regenerated
I myself first must be.

A Chinese General